For Mum, Bethany and Katie, who pieces of me....

Summer 2006

Staring out across the Ionian Sea. From our privileged position high up on a rocky mountain we can see the deep blue ocean. I can make out small glints of white as the waves reflect back from the hot sun.

I can see thick green forests and small villages, rocky tracks and unmade roads. If I stare hard I can make out small figures on the seafront running onto the white sands.

Mark and I are looking out from the infinity pool. A section at the front has a large glass viewing area perfect for watching and relaxing. I am propped up against the side of the pool on my elbows, he is treading water.

We smile at each other as we take in the view. It is quiet, we are the only visitors to the swimming pool this afternoon, and all I can hear is the hum of crickets and the quiet sound of a classical tune in the breeze floating out from the pool bar.

In the cool water it's a magnificent contrast from the ferocious heat.

Mark moves from treading water and swims behind me.

He holds his strong arms around me and kisses my neck, I feel the water trickle off his hair onto mine and down my neck. He moves his hands down my back sending little blasts off electric all over my body. He reaches across my chest and inside my bikini. I close my eyes and let my head roll back against his shoulder.

Suddenly Mark is moving away from me, cutting the water, his shoulders rising up and down, expert butterfly stroke and little splashing. He stops and turns around, standing in the shallows, waving at me. He raises his arms up above his head, and appears to be showing me something. It's my bikini.

I will be making my way back to the side topless…..again. His favourite little tease. I laugh as he walks back to our sun loungers.

Following him I swim in the same direction and Mark throws my bikini back to me, so I can re dress myself from the privacy of the water. I needn't feel shy, there is only the barman here and he is mixing and sipping drinks.

Bikini re-applied I sit on the concrete steps of the pool, submerged to my waistline, with my arms stretched out behind me. I smirk to myself, Mark is taking pictures of me as I pose, sun tanned and toned body against a white o,neil halter neck. I am forever his muse. I enjoy his attention.

Back on the sun loungers we lay side by side. Sipping some pink cocktails with elaborate umbrellas. My towel is soft and smells of lotion as I lay forward into it. I let my mind drift and slip slowly into sleep, my hand in Marks.

"Ruth" he whispers "mmmmmm" I reply quietly from within my snooze. "you were amazing last night, like an animal."

I giggle to myself, open one eye and raise my head back up to see him grinning back at me.

Last night we had gone down into the town. My memory is hazy, there was food, we met up with another couple, we danced on tables and smashed plates. I seem to recall being in a large outside nightclub, big thumping beats and flaming sambuca shots.

It must have been getting light when we all finally stumbled back up the dusty path back to the hotel.

Back in our room Mark and I had turning on music, opened some wine and carried on partying.

I had pinned him down and ripped off his clothes. I can remember him tying me up in the shirt I had ripped from his back, until I had rolled over and got the better of him.

I recall he stopped fighting me and let me take over control as I forced his muscled arms with my knees, kissing his face and his chest and slowly further down.

Back on the sun loungers we are hungover but happy. I squeeze his hand and turn up the corners of my mouth in amusement.

We both lie back down and doze off in the sun. It feels good.

Summer 1997 onwards

It is easy to look back to the start of a relationship with rose tinted spectacles and say that there were no faults or weaknesses and that everything was perfect. That as a couple you never argued, had harsh words or took the other person for granted.

What I feel would be more realistic is that if I said my relationship with Mark was never any of those things.

We did argue, sometimes we even fought. We were each other's harshest critics. But we were also each other's protectors and keepers, and because of those very real faults', which we both accepted within each other, along with all of our strengths, we had the foundations of an immense partnership.

We had what I still maintain was our version of perfect.

I was only 17 when Mark and I met, he was 18.

We were at a party in the pub where I worked.

Gangs of girls clad in hot pants and push up bra tops showing off to groups of boys in designer checked shirts guzzling cider and alcopops.

Looking back now, like a window through time, I can see the brightly coloured eyeshadow, and massive bouffant hairstyle. I can almost smell the cheap perfume. I wore a blue halter neck top, and a long white skirt, which split almost to my waist.

The pub had a traditional, country style, with lots of wooden beams and seating areas. It was tired though. I recall the tables and chairs had a tacky feel , many years of spilt drinks creating a film around the cheap pine. The rooms all smelled of acrid burnt chip fat and cigarette smoke, an almost blue tinge to the air and stained yellow glass in the windows.

The function room had an enormous grey stone fireplace and its own private bar area, where we were all taking it in turns to pour rounds of shots, colourless liqueur which would be the catalyst to the mother of all hangovers the following day.

At the time when we first Mark was my best friends boyfriend. I had a boyfriend of my own too.

But there was just something between us. When we spoke to each other over the loud music, standing so close together to hear, I could feel him breathe on my cheek, and sparks of electricity went down my neck and into my spine. As we spoke we held each others gaze, our eyes hazel mirroring.

At end of the night Mark took my friend home in his car, and I must have stumbled home with my boyfriend to get some sleep before my Sunday dinner shift back at the pub. Running food to tables I was distracted by thoughts of Mark.

Some weeks later my friend mentioned that Mark wanted to take her scuba diving as he was an instructor, and asked me to go along too. Whilst I thought this sounded very exciting and encouraged her to go she couldn't bear the thought of him seeing her in her swimming costume. I offered to go along with her for morale support. I knew, even then, that I had another motive. I was confident in my body image at the time and didn't feel threatened by the depths of the swimming pool. I was a strong swimmer and knew I got positive attention in a swimsuit, but the reality was I just wanted to see Mark again.

By the time it was the actual night we were all supposed to be going diving, Mark and my friend had broken up, but she said that it was fine with her that I went with him anyway.

It turned out was fairly terrible at the diving part, panicking about cleaning my mask properly, and concentrating on how to breathe in the darkness of the under water.

Mark taught me special hand gestures that we could use below the surface to say if I was OK, needed to go up, or sink further down, I watched him smiling at me, his grin around the mouthpiece of his mask. It was strange being at the bottom of the deep pool, with just our new sign language and the clicks of the breathing apparatus.

When our session was finished Mark helped me to unfasten the straps of the weight jacket. His strong and nimble fingers unclipping the ties across my chest, brushing my breasts and apologising and blushing as he looked down at me. I don't think Mark was sorry he had touched me that way and I wasn't either. The electricity had passed between us again, almost taking my breath away.

We talked all the way home, as he drove, about anything, and everything. Nothing was off the table and he was such fun to be around.

We were only very young, but we were suddenly spending so much time together, increasing cinema trips, evening drives and days out, I took Mark to every house party I went to.

I was a socialite and a terrible party animal, drinking and making a fool of myself, singing, dancing on tables, even stripping at times. Mark disapproved and tried to calm me, wanting to protect me from any harm, and being furious with me for embarrassing him.

It was a pattern that would continue into our adult life. Mark carrying me home when I was drunk, holding me up when I fell down, paying bills when I made debts and protecting me from dangers I had sometimes created for myself.

At 6 foot 1 with broad strong shoulders Mark completely dwarfed my tiny 5 foot frame. But his dominance and attitude made me feel safe. I should mention that with this demeanour came aggression, and his desire to control me. This is where our fights would start. Even when we were both still in our teens we would jockey for the top position with one another.

By the time I was in the final months of my A levels Mark had moved into a small semi detached house in the village where my college was and I started staying there a few nights a week with him. Far from luxurious the property was unloved. The carpet worn bare in places, floral and sticky lino in the kitchen and always cold. We were plagued my smells of fish that came and went in particular in the front bedroom. We would joke we felt like someone was watching us in the night, and towels which we hung at the top of the stairs were forever at the bottom moments later...it should have given us the creeps but instead we felt the opposite.

I would make us simple dinners of salad and potatoes or some sort of cheap casserole and we would sit and watch TV on an inflatable sofa, because we couldn't afford any proper furniture. Sometimes the power ran out in the meter part way through our programme, and we were plunged into silence and darkness, but we didn't care, we were alone to do what we liked, with no parents or rules, and spent many a happy passionate evening entertaining ourselves.

I can fondly remember one morning, we had an intimate lie in, experimenting with pleasures I had never felt before.

Afterwards we had had a bath together, cramped in the white tin, surrounded by steam and bubbles, and then we were getting dried, sharing scratchy towels that marked our skin, and laughing.

We stood in the bedroom about to dress and Mark looked down to me with a very serious intention written across his face, he simply said "one day I'm going to marry you Ruth"

I melted inside, a warm and intense heat all over my body, from my toes to my flushing cheeks. Looking into each eyes as he said those words.

Later Years

I passed my A Levels and started a career in the local town in retail management. Mark passed his apprenticeship and became a fully-fledged electrician. We moved to a flat in the town where I worked. It surely wasn't glamorous. We shared three small rooms. Jam packed with everything we owned.

Marks car got broken into constantly, as did his works van. The not knowing what state the vehicles would be in when we opened the curtains in a morning was frustrating. Then there was the noise of people and traffic, I struggled sleeping, in the urban bustle away from the quiet rural existence I had grown up in.

We would lie awake listening to revellers coming back from town, screaming, shouting, swearing at all hours most days of the week. Someone even tried our door once. Mark leapt out of bed and was stood behind it with a baseball bat in his hand.

The bathroom could barely occupy one full sized adult and was usually covered in various patterns of mould. It was a lottery for warm water in the shower, and the damp curtain would wrap itself around me whenever I tried to wash my hair, any arm movements causing me to get tangled.

The environment heavily incentivised us and within less than a year we had saved the deposit to buy a house, and we bought our first home, a little semi-detached house in a smaller village, a few miles out of town.

As an animal lover I persuaded Mark our life was empty without pets and we got two rabbits, and I moved my pony Barney from a field near my parents' house to a nearby livery stable.

The little house was buried in old fashioned 60's style decor, with huge patterned and flowery wallpaper in every room. We went around the house making it our own, re-tiling, painting, and even gardening. Sometimes Mark would paint my nose to tease me, and I would paint his arm, we would keep splashing blobs of colour at each other, eventually falling to the floor, removing each other's paint-stained clothes.

Over the years I became very close to Marks family, they were warm and inviting, easy to spend time with, and friendly. There was always a BBQ on someone's garden, or a meal out at restaurants, they all liked spending time with each other, and I embraced this. I was particularly close to Mark's, mum, Carol, with her often saying I was the daughter she never had.

In the Christmas of 2000 I was in the stock room of the shoe department I was managing. I was halfway up a ladder trying to sticker barcodes on to heels ready for the boxing day sale. One of my assistants said that I was desperately needed on the shop floor. I can remember heading out of the stock room, angrily ramming my hands into my pockets, irritated at being disturbed. As I made my way out of the dark stock area to the bright lights of the shop floor, I could see Mark sat in one of the chairs smiling. He stood to greet me, and my anger ebbed away. I was pleased he had come to visit me and smiled up at him.

Mark got down on one knee right there and then. He produced a small red box from behind his back, and slowly opened it, his fingers trembling. The box revealed a gold ring with a large diamond, and two smaller diamonds set either side. He quietly asked me to marry him, asking simply if I would spend the rest of my life with him. Surrounded by festive shoppers and colleagues I said yes as he placed the ring on my finger. He lifted me up off the floor and swung me around, I felt like a fairytale princess, wrapped in our own bubble of adoration.

We didn't make any immediate wedding plans, instead concentrating time and finances on our home.

Mark and I also added to our furry family, as after turning up in the middle of the night at a friend of a friends, we got our first cat, Pharaoh. She needed a home, and Mark had said that he didn't really like cats, but when a playful little ball of black fur curled up on his knee or followed him around with her toy mice for hours on end he soon forgot his reservations. Within a year we got our first dog. We got Mia from a rescue sanctuary. She was a 16-week-old Doberman cross Staffie which sounds like possibly quite a mean dog, but Mia was the kindest and sweetest and very loving. She was loyal from the start, and we looked after her like a baby. Mark was completely smitten with her.

We enjoyed many a Sunday afternoon, with me riding Barney and Mark walking alongside us with Mia, who would trot along next to him, proud to be with her favourite person.

I never lost my passion for all things horses, and Mark, albeit begrudgingly at times, accepted this.

Cars were also a big part of our lives. If it had wheels Mark had to modify it. His obsession started with his old Volkswagen Jetta and my battered and rusting Vauxhall Nova, but soon progressed to the slightly newer VW Golf and Polo. Mark would spend hours outside at the weekends, washing and polishing his pride and joy. There were exhausts and neon lights and dump valves galore.

As Marks enthusiasm grew he progressed to buying a buying a much newer and more powerful car, a silver Toyota Supra. We would go out for drives on a summers evening, going faster and faster as the countryside got swallowed up as we went round bend after bend. Looking back now it was perhaps careless, but with the wind in my hair and Mark at the wheel it felt how we should be.

In 2005 we made some more adventurous changes. I managed to persuade Mark that I needed another horse now Barney was getting on a bit, and my little black beauty came into our lives. She was only a yearling when we got her and was quite small and in poor condition. It surprised us just how much she grew when we fed her and cared for her properly. She became a large and strong with a temper to match.

I could spend hours attempting to command her, until I was soaked with sweat and covered in dirt and fur. Mark would watch on witnessing my frustrations, but then when he asked anything of this same horse it seemed to me that she would obey instantly.

It was also the Summer of 2005 that we travelled to Santorini in Greece to be married. We took the whole family. Both sets of parents, siblings, and some grandparents, whoever wanted to come was welcome.

Greece had become a favourite holiday location for Mark and I, so it was very fitting that on the 30th July 2005 we stood on a cliff in a winery, and said I do.

We got married at 6pm in the evening but the sun was still beating down on us, it was the day I had always dreamed of, married in the blazing sun, high up over the crashing waves with the man that I loved. Dressed in my dusted rose wedding dress I sipped celebration wine, with Mark and I grinning at each other and the family as we posed for photograph after photograph in the idyllic setting. The celebrations carried on at a local tavern, and went on well into the night, and the following morning, with us all quaffing champagne, until it got dark and then light again.

The following summer we were met with some serious challenges.

Mark and I were leaving our street to go to the livery yard to see Barney, with Mia in the car with us, as we pulled out, we were almost wiped out by a silver sports car doing what we supposed was well over a hundred miles an hour. We both remarked to each other over the driver's stupidity, as we pulled out of the street heading off along a country road in the same direction as the speeding car.

As we got around the corner we were met by carnage. A small blue car was in the middle of the road, every single part of it crushed. The silver sports car was face down in a ditch nearby. There was smoke in the air, which was all the tiny particles of paint where the vehicles had collided. There was a moment where all was silent, and time seemed to stand still.

Mark and I left Mia in the car and instinctively ran to the small blue car, or the wreckage that was left of it. The couple who were in the front seats were barely conscious. I started to call for an ambulance. A woman was running up behind me, who had come from a nearby farm saying she had already dialled three nines, I ignored her. I could already see before me that Mark was forcing his way into the back seat of the mangled blue car, and underneath the debris was a little boy, who was moaning. He had blood all over his face and was covered in glass. As Mark tried to comfort him, I noticed the little boy's leg. His femoral artery was cut, and thick, dark blood was oozing down his leg and pooling on what was left of the car seats. I heard my voice on the phone to the emergency services, it sounded calm, almost measured from the hysteria I felt inside "You must send a fire engine with cutting gear, there is a little boy in this vehicle and if you don't send a fire engine to cut him out he is going to die"

The little boy was lucky, they did send a fire engine, they also sent the air ambulance and he made a full recovery. His parents suffered broken bones and I expect some haunting dreams, but they also made a full recovery. The uninjured sports car driver got a mere fine.

Mark however remained traumatised from the accident and dealing with the little boy, and a few months later he was diagnosed with type 1 diabetes. The consultants said that he was probably always going to develop it, but the accident had been the catalyst for him getting it then.

Mark lost a lot of weight and had to spend quite a period of time off work, learning to manage his illness and constant insulin injections and testing of blood sugar levels.

But Mark strong as ever battled through and came out fighting, stronger, albeit angrier, yet pleasing all the consultants and nurses with his progress and his ability to cope with his illness like it had always been a part of him.

The last of the series of challenges was a good one. Mark found a blue Persian cross cat outside the Doctors surgery one night after a check-up. It was a bitter cold night and when he brought the cat home it looked as if it was on its last legs. Starving, bony, almost skeletal, and very knotty fur. He looked every bit as if he needed a good home. So that's what we gave him, and Teddy joined the furry family.

In the winter of 2007 we sold our little house, and made a move to another nearby village, to a large detached house with a big garden. We made a sizeable amount of money on our first home, and our families recommended that we re-invested some of this money into our new house to keep our mortgage payments down. Ever the gamblers Mark and I ignored this advice. To us life was for living. Right there in the moment, that's how we existed. Mark bought a Mitsubishi Evolution and we had a bespoke designed kitchen, new carpets throughout and a water bed.

It's fair to say we behaved as materialistic people and knew what we liked and wanted; sadly, we didn't heed the recommendations of those around us.

By this time Mark had worked his way up the employment ladder and was now a contracts manager for the firm he had worked for all his adult life, and I had been promoted at the IT company that I worked for, earning hundreds of pounds in commission every month, money didn't feel like a concern to us.

In all ways, emotionally, physically and with our possessions and animals around us we continued to build our castle.

Fall from Grace

During Christmas 2008, my pony Barney had to be put to sleep.

He had suffered with a short illness. As the vet held a pipe to his nose he struggled to breathe and choked, his eyes looked over the vets shoulder and into mine. I knew what he was telling me.

Somewhere in a place far away the vet was giving me more treatment options, factoring in chances of survival. I put my hands out and grabbed her, pleaded with her to stop talking. Enough.Its time.

Mark and I were both there when it happened, and just like ever he was my rock, ready to catch me as I fell.

He arranged for Barney to be taken away and cremated.

But I fell hard. At work and with friends I would put on a brave face, acting like I was coping, but at the weekends when I had time to think, I missed Barney so much it almost consumed me. Only Mark really knew how hard I was finding life, and he put all his efforts into helping me to train Lazer so that I could have with her, what I had lost when Barney died.

When valentine's day came round, I was still an emotional wreck. Mark bought me a dozen red roses and placed them over Barneys ashes. There was a card too, reading:

Mum, thanks for believing in me and giving me the best life I could ever have hoped for! Now go and do with the black one what you did with me, she wants to learn! I will see you again in many years time……..

I got that far reading the card before I went blind with tears and dropped to the floor, Mark catching me and holding me in his arms, having written those words, knowing me that deeply, and being brave enough to put it down on paper. In those darkest hours Mark saved me from drowning in my own grief.

The training did not go exactly to plan. Although we sent Lazer away to a professional yard for her to be backed for riding she came back not how I expected. Lazer was very strong willed and opinionated. Mark wanted to help me, but he had never really ridden much before and Lazer was a freshly backed horse and therefore not a beginner's ride. In the summer of 2009 I had a bad fall as she took off with me, I was knocked unconscious and permanently damaged my back, resulting in many sessions with physiotherapists and osteopaths.

As usual Mark was there to pick up the pieces, encouraging me to find another trainer to help me with my challenging mare, and pushing me onwards.

At the end of the same summer there was trouble at the company I worked for. John and Jane were Man and Wife and were joint directors of the firm. Jane accused John of having an affair with a colleague, a young girl in the sales team and the scandal affected everyone in the office.

She was perhaps 21 years old, blonde, buxom and fluttering eyelashes, she wore tight pencil skirts, and revealing blouses, but also had a confident presence about her. I could certainly see the appeal. I admit I did question her myself as to the goings on. She replied that John was old enough to be her father and whilst she realised her actions were inappropriate it was harmless fun. I can recall at the time pondering over it in my own head, confused as to what, and who to believe.

John and I would often need to be out of the office together to attend customer meetings. Alone in his car we would use the time to talk about issues in the office or how to help clients with problems. John then used this discussion time to confide in me that he suspected Jane was playing away, and that is why she had accused him first, almost as a diversion and cover up. I didn't really know what to think. I certainly didn't think it was normal behaviour within a company, and resented being dragged into the disputes between all parties.

One day when there was just John and I in the boardroom he confessed that his curiosity had eventually got the better of him, and he had been snooping through Jane's mobile phone. He discovered lots of calls and texts to one unknown number. He asked me what he should do, and I joked that we should call it.

Sat at the big desks with the conference calling facility, we had our hands pinned under our knees with intrepid anticipation, John punched the numbers in….it rang….Mark answered. My world spun.

I stormed out, into the privacy and darkness of one of the corridors. This wasn't a game I wanted to play. John swiftly joined me, he said that it was clear that Mark and Jane had been meeting up in secret. I couldn't quite believe what I was hearing, as he marched up and down the hallway, arms folded across his chest, crinkling his suit. I had my arms across my own chest, and was teetering off balance in my high heeled shoes. I remember feeling like I was going to pop with anger and running back into the offices.

I called Mark from my desk, shaking as I punched the numbers into the phone "Mark you know I love you very much don't you?"'…I struggled as soon as I started to speak, not sure how this sort of a conversation should go. I was totally unprepared. "Yes I do " Mark replied hastily and quietly on the other end of the phone. "I think I know what this is about Ruth" So maybe Jane had called him, tipped him off I suspected, a warning in advance, but I didn't say anything to Mark "Really?" I raged, "how dare you embarrass me like this, in front of all my colleagues, what the hell is going on! "I shrieked. "Wait at the office" said Mark "I am coming over to see you"

We met in the office car park. Waiting for Mark to arrive had seemed like an eternity. My imagination conjuring up various scenarios as I sat on the stone steps outside, suddenly unable to talk to anyone else within the four walls of the office.

Marks Truck pulled up and I took a deep breath and opened the passenger door. We drove away from all the prying eyes.

Sat in a wooded carpark, he explained how Jane had sent him an email from her company email address to his work email address, asking if I had mentioned anything going on between my colleague, and my boss John. How Jane had been distraught, they had ended up calling each other and texting each other and had actually met up several times in secret, when he had told me he was elsewhere. I was shocked and furious, but far worse than that I felt betrayed by Mark. I had never had a good relationship with Jane, who was domineering, rude and confrontational towards me on a daily basis, and now I really felt that Mark had given her the ultimate one upmanship. She clicked her fingers and he obeyed, and she knew it was all behind my back.

He explained to me that there was nothing in it, that they were just friends, and he had somehow been drawn into supporting her in her hours of need, sworn to secrecy.

It was a strange time for me, because whilst I did believe Mark, and also Jane, who I questioned about her actions, I believed some of what they were saying, that there was nothing in their relationship other than friendship, I was scared by how easy he had found it to keep the truth from me, lie about where he was all the time, and clearly enjoyed the thrill of the chase. I also found the content of some of their text messages un-nerving, they were suggestive and flirtatious.

Mark was my rock, not Jane's. I still very much needed him.

Things were awkward and strained between us for a long time. The sale's girl was paid off and she took the money and left quietly and moved on to make a fresh start elsewhere. John and Jane got back on with their lives together. The business kept turning. I locked away any remaining feelings of insecurity, refusing to give them airtime.

In the Autumn of that year we got Mia a new playmate, another dog joined the furry brood, Phoenix, who was rescued by the RSPCA. Phoenix was a crazy tan and white whirlwind, a staffie crossed with some sort of Zebedee, seen only as a blur of speed to begin with! He had bags of energy and was a welcome distraction.

This wasn't the end of upheaval though.

In March 2010 our cat Teddy was run over and killed outside the house. I was out on a works dinner when it happened.

I got home to find Mark waiting for me at the bottom of the stairs in his dressing gown, his head in his hands, knowing how destroyed I would be.

Teddy was in a box in the garage, he had died straight away. Angry and alcohol fuelled I blamed one of our female neighbours who always drove too fast, I threatened I was going to go to the house then, in the middle of the night, and ask her what she had done. I screamed and cried and lashed out at Mark, furious with him for making me put Teddy out that morning, unable to accept that this was happening, I was like a wild animal, screeching and clawing, until he shook me so hard I nearly fainted.

Mark wouldn't let me see Teddy that night; he got him out the following morning. He had carefully turned Teddy's head to one side so I couldn't see the horrific damage the accident had caused. Once again Mark was protecting me as best as he could.

Teddy looked beautiful, like he was sleeping, his lovely fluffy blue grey fur filling the large cardboard box. Mark and I sat in the kitchen with our dead cat between us and wept.

Once again, I struggled to cope with loss. Whereas with Barney I hadn't had the energy and fight, and Mark kept scooping me up, this time I was angry and suffered terrible mood swings. I knew I was difficult to live with at that time.

Mark suggested to me that he thought I had bi-polar disorder, getting pages up on the internet, showing them to me, saying, "Look this is you?! This is what you are like!" I recall reading the description of the pages he had been studying, questioning myself, wondering if it were true.

There was also a further commotion when his brother Martyn announced that he and his wife Joanna were expecting their first child. I was overjoyed for them, and made no secret of it, but Mark raged at his parents, accusing them of forcing the pair into having children too young. It was clear to me at the time that Mark was jealous that this wasn't our announcement, he had made no secret of his desire to have children, and I had been holding us back. I knew that his anger was mis-directed. I worried there would be repercussions.

By April 2010 I believed our relationship was in recovery. Although we had been thrown some difficult challenges, we had weathered the worst of the storm. We went out to parties, restaurants and made holiday plans. We spent time together at the house and out walking with the dogs. We fell back into our old ways, our passionate selves, capable of a good argument, but always an equal reconciliation to match.

I can fondly remember a works night out in early May, I stood in our kitchen waiting to leave that evening, with my sparkly silver dress, and my hair up in curls. Mark came down the stairs in his dinner suit, and his eyes lit up when he saw me. "You look just like a beautiful fairy Ruth" he smiled and stroked my shoulders.

At the event there was a five course dinner and drinks and dancing, the wine flowed and we both stumbled into the house in the early hours of the morning, with helium balloons tied to our arms, laughing as we fell through our front door.

I was in the bathroom taking off my make-up when Mark ambushed me with a water pistol, chasing me around the house, with me giggling, before pinning me to the bed, with lust in his eyes.

At that time I had no idea we were anything other than happy.

The start of the end

Mark received an unknown friend request from a social networking site.

I was in the bathroom, and he was in the office room, next door, on the computer, and shouted across the landing to me "Ruth, do you know the surname of that Tracey who keeps her horse with yours?" There were several women who kept horses at the yard, and although I could picture her face, I didn't know her surname.

"I don't think so, no, I've never asked. Why?" I replied, not really listening, I was enjoying a good soak in the bubbles with some candles.

"She has sent me a friend request I think, well at least I think it's her, it's a blonde Tracey that looks like her, so I assume it's her, I will just add her then?" Mark was explaining, seeking my approval.

"OK" I shouted back, lying back against the back of the white bath, only just able to see ever the sea of bubbles as they surrounded me.

That should have been the end of it...only it wasn't. Because it wasn't the same Tracey.

It was a woman who lived a little way down our street.

She and her husband were part of a local dog breeding programme and had seen Mark walking our dogs when they were out with their pointers. Or there was another version of the same story where she had seen his works van and taken some of the details off it...as I think about these explanations; in retrospect none of them really made sense.

But the reality is, Mark and Tracey started walking the dogs together in an evening every few days or so. This was good for her husband, because he worked long hours, and I guess good for me, because I could my time in an evening working and playing with my horses without anyone wondering when I would be home.

The truth was that I was spending more time with the horses trying to get success, but not really achieving what I wanted. Lazers strong will grew and grew, and I had become a little afraid of her both on her back, and on the ground. Without Mark there I didn't feel as confident, and she knew it, barging me and dominating me at any given chance. Lazer had become large and very strong built. I could no longer see over her back, and her head towered above mine. I was small and felt fragile next to her. Charlie was not as dominant, but as an ex-racehorse he had more psychological problems then I had first realised. He was terrified of being shut in his stable, or tied up, or any activity that represented being captive or confined. The things that scared him sent him into a furious panic. He was tall and athletic, orange by colour and temperament. The two horses were great stable mates for each other, but too challenging for me to cope with.

All of a sudden I had gone from a naughty little pony to two huge horses, and I was out of my depth but wouldn't admit it.

So more time to be at the horses yard, whilst struggling, but at least whilst ever Mark was with Tracey he wasn't watching me fail over and over again at something I wanted so badly.

I did however consider thus was a call to arms, and over time started to realise that I should be making more of an effort to walk the dogs with Mark, both to see him and them, so I started alternating what I did at evenings and weekends. I felt guilt over the amount of time I dedicated to my equine buddies.

I can distinctly recall the last day I suggested we walk them together, calling him from the office.

It was a beautiful warm evening, and I thought it would be lovey to walk down the nature trail together, chatting and throwing the ball for the dogs, and as I had sat at my desk daydreaming about it, in my mind, I was almost there already.

"Hey Mark, I don't think I will ride tonight. I think I will come and walk the dogs with you instead?"

"Oh no, that's OK, I fancy going on my own with them anyway, you always walk slow" his reply took me aback.

Disappointed, I tried again

"Oh, come on Mark it will be nice in the warm sun, I promise I won't walk too slow"

"No Ruth, you go to the horses, I want to go on my own and I don't really want to talk about it"

I felt a little hurt, but I guessed he had his reasons, perhaps a stressful day, maybe he needed some head space. I would talk to him about it when we got home, asked what had gone wrong, or what his problem was...

I had a great ride on Lazer and felt more confident than normal. I even rode Charlie for a while afterwards. The heat had beat down on us and I made an attempt to tidy myself up before I went home, shaking fur out of my clothes, and wiping sweat and dried sand from my face.

I smiled to myself as I fed the horses, thinking ahead to my own dinner, and hoping to talk to Mark about what was bothering him..........

26th May 2010

Driving back to the house with all the car windows open, it was warm for May, and I was enjoying it. The sunshine peeping through the sunroof and warming the top of my head. Summer was beginning.

I could almost taste the dinner I was about to start cooking, and hoped we would maybe pop out on to the garden afterwards for a nice glass of red wine.

This is what summer should be all about, after a long day at work, letting my hair down out of a pony tail, and sitting outside, swinging in a chair and letting my toes run through the grass.

As I came to the top of the street, I looked to see if Mark was coming back up the trail with the dogs yet, but I couldn't see him. All I noticed was a slim blonde woman walking off down the trail, with her hound. She was wearing hot pants and a vest top, and was walking away with pace and purpose.

I pulled on to the drive and locked the car, Pharoah cat came running over to greet me, meowing, and rolling around in the grit and dirt on the doorstep and showing me her tummy.

I went into the house, and the hall way was dark and cool, it was nice to take off my boots and socks and step across the cold tiles.

I went into the kitchen and started planning tea properly, getting bottles of spices and onions out of cupboards. Searching through the rack I found a lovely looking red wine.

The front door banged and both dogs came bounding in, pleased to see me and have a fuss, they were panting and ran to their water bowl, slurping loudly and making little puddles as they clumsily drank their fill.

Mark came in behind them and took off his walking boots and walked into the kitchen.

I looked at his face and knew something was far from right. His cheeks were ashen in colour and his eyes looked flat as if there was no light or life in them. As I looked up at him I realised he had lost some weight again, Mark looked gaunt and drawn. He kept gulping and swallowing as if there wasn't enough air for him, and was pacing the kitchen.

He opened the cupboard and got out a tall glass and filled it with water straight from the tap. He drank it all, and then filled the glass again. The pacing and gulping and struggling was starting to scare me….

"Is everything ok?" I asked. He didn't reply he just glared at me, almost as if I wasn't there.

"Mark what is it?" again, nothing, just a hollow look back, with a cold stare. I began to wonder if I had done something wrong, was he going to berate me, or start yelling? I felt my hackles rising.

"Have you done something with Tracey?" I joked, imagining her enormous husband angrily pelting the door with his fists demanding to come in our house. Still no response from Mark.

"Have you done something with Tracey that will make her husband angry?" again I teased.

"Yes" Mark said. And there it was, all of a sudden, my joke felt very wrong.

A freezing tickle rushed over me, I felt as if someone had just poured the coldest of liquids slowly all over my body, and a feeling of nausea sat in the very pit of my stomach. I started to shake. In my worst nightmares I would not have imagined he would have answered what had started as a jovial question with such a frank and honest answer. So real. I was completely taken aback.

I felt as if I was far away, as if in the second tier of a theatre, watching a scene played out before me. Like my head was miles from my body. I saw my small hands shaking, trying to grasp hold of each other and keep still. My tongue felt enormous in my mouth, like a blockage to stop any words coming out.

"Have you slept with her?" I tried to ask, my voice coming out very small and weak, trembling.

"No" Mark replied, I didn't know if he was still gulping at this moment, because I couldn't bring myself to even look at him. I was afraid of the truth I might see.

"Have you touched each other or something?" I tried asking a different question in the hopes of a different answer, maybe even a different outcome. "No" he replied...it was like some sort of horrendous guessing game, Mark giving nothing away, and me having to pull the information out of him. I knew eventually I would ask a question to which I could not bear to hear the answer to.

"Have you kissed her?" I asked him, but this time I looked up at him, at his face, way up above mine, him standing more than a whole foot taller than me, but it was as if his face was somewhere in the sky, far, far away, and I could not reach it. We were stood only a few feet apart, I could see the sweat now, running down his brow, and the trauma ran lines right across his pale face.

"Yes" he eventually replied. The cold feeling within me suddenly became worse, I felt as if was pressing down on me, forcing me in and I was somehow drowning in an invisible liquid. I grabbed hold of the kitchen work top and steadied myself. A million thoughts and questions were going through my head, but I couldn't seem to think of, or process words that would go together and make a sentence.

"Are you in love with her?" was all my now feeble mouth could manage to ask "I don't know Ruth, I don't even know her, I don't know how I feel about her yet."

I looked over to the central worktop, where the two wine glasses sat, next to the un-opened wine. The thick icy feeling that was trying to drown me turned slightly warmer and for a split second I found the strength to shoot across the kitchen, pushed past Mark and open the bottle, needily, and frantically.

I wanted my poison as quick as I could get it. The glasses lay redundant on the worktop, and I started gulping the warm red wine straight from the bottle as fast as I could, praying that I could just make this all go away. I broke away from the wine and loudly placed the bottle back on to the solid granite worktop, but I kept my fingers well wrapped around the neck. I wouldn't let go until I had drunk every last drop.

"What was it like to kiss her?" I asked, braver now with courage from the wine. I didn't wait for the answer. "Is she a better kisser than me?" I was terrified of the answers to these questions. I was brave enough to ask them, but I would not be bold enough to cope with their answers. Yet still I kept hounding Mark "Did it feel better than when we are kissing?" that's an improvement, I thought, my voice was slightly more assertive and less like a pathetic whisper.

"It just felt different that's all Ruth, it just felt good to be feeling someone else lips, doing different things, with someone else."

Predictably his answers crucified me, killing me inside. The cold feeling was back. It wanted to take me down. I had no strength, my legs didn't want to carry me.

I looked up at Mark again. The man who I always went to for help and love and support, and so suddenly he was lost to me. His face was pale and grey, and his eyes gave nothing away. He was gulping for air again, like a fish going along the top of the water in its tank.

"I'm leaving you" and that was all that he said as he walked out of the kitchen and into the lounge.

A cold tidal wave washed all over me, hitting my face first, then down my arms to my fingertips, down my legs to my toes so I could barely stand, it felt as if a Mark was slowly drowning me with the few words that he had said.

I sank to the tiles. I still had the wine bottle in one hand, and I swigged some more, as I dropped to the floor hoping that some warmth could be found in the dark liquor.

I had lain on the floor for some time, staring into nothing, my vision blank. I rolled from my back on to my stomach and propped myself onto my hands and knees. Eventually I picked myself up, almost crawling along the tiles for a way, and got into the dining room, which lead into the lounge.

Normally stepping off the cold tiles on to the warm carpets was a pleasant feeling, but not then, at that moment all external sensation in my body was lost, all I could feel was nausea and faint, the bile rising in my throat as an emotional knife twisted in my stomach, the blade slicing flesh, slowly killing me as the cold liquid poured through every vein.

Mark was sat on the far-right side of the sofa. I sat on the far left. Two people who were normally sat so close together were now so far apart.

"Mark you can't leave me your my world" I pleaded.

"I have to Ruth. I have to try and be happy, I need to be. I have been unhappy for some time now." And suddenly all of Marks worries came tumbling out, how he felt trapped by the house, the mortgage, the bills and finances, his work, my work, but worst of all he felt trapped by me. He didn't just want to be with me, he wanted to be with other women, to know what they felt like and tasted like and experience sensual feelings with other people.

Whilst this truth was gushing out of him I started to get to the bottom of the bottle of red wine. As I took the last mouthful and swallowed sediment the red poison was all I could focus on.

I drifted off into memories as I recalled once when we were 18 years old and hadn't been a couple very long. Mark had taken me to Gran Canaria, it was the first time I had left the country without my parents and siblings. We spent an entire fortnight eating and drinking and making love. It was blissful.

At the end of the two weeks we were waiting for the transfer coach and Mark had said to me "when we get back I think we should both see other people. I don't think there should be just us, I want to meet other woman and see what it's like, I feel too young to settle down. I will still see you sometimes, but I won't come to your house every night after work anymore, I won't always be with you"

I remembered how shocked I was, but didn't know what to say and how once we were back in England, I had cried myself to sleep after he had dropped me off at my parents' house and drove away.

Two days later Mark had decided it has been a terrible mistake, and after having spoken to his mother and Aunty he told me that we were meant to be together, and he was nothing without me.

As I put the empty bottle of wine on to the coffee table I decided that this was probably a more adult version of the same feelings, possibly harboured from way back then.

"It's not like it was when we were 18 you know Mark? Everyone is married off and has children now, it's not just a big game anymore. We are supposed to be together, and grow old together"

I hoped as I was saying this that he may reconsider how he felt.

"Well, that's not what's happening now. Talking to Tracey and being with her over these past few weeks has made me realise, like when I was sat outside the garage last Sunday and you were at the horses all day and I was alone. I thought this isn't right, I should be with someone who I can spend my time with, someone like her."

I felt guilty and considered maybe I had left Mark lonely. But I also felt anger towards this woman.

"So it's basically Tracey has turned you against me then? She will regret this, when she is burning in hell, and her husband will know all about it, when I write that she is a whore and a slut all over her god damned hairdressers' car"

That was better the cold feeling had decided to subside so I could be angry, this was how I could survive.

I ran to the hallway and put on my trainers, and grabbed my phone and car keys, and slammed the front door behind me.

I don't know how long Mark and I had been inside talking, but it was much cooler and fresher outside and almost dark.

I started to walk out of our close and off down the street towards Tracey's house. The wine was taking effect now, and the cold, dying feeling inside of me had been replaced by a woozy feeling, and I wobbled and stumbled. As I got towards

Tracey's house, I realised I could just knock on the door and tell her husband what had been going on, how his wife was a manipulative creature, who tricks other women's husbands into thinking they don't love their wives, and the life that they have with them.

I stopped outside the house, with my car key in my hand feeling really tempted to write on the car. Really tempted to knock on her door and punch her in the face. Make her pay for what she had done to me as I drifted off into my thoughts, I started to wonder what happened to women who knock on doors and punch people and vandalise cars? Did I care? Would I go to prison? Would she fight back? Or would I get a good first blow and knock her to the ground? I imagined what it would be like to laugh at her writhing around on the floor as I stood above her.

Before I realised what I was doing, I had walked past Tracey's house, past the end of the street, over the roundabout and towards the woods, I didn't know how that had happened. I felt confused.

It was late, and beyond the streetlights it was pitch black. I was still only dressed in my jodhpurs and a t shirt, but the alcohol kept me warm.

I was annoyed with myself for walking so far without thinking about it and I started to walk back towards the street…. marching towards Tracey's house, not caring about writing all over the fancy soft top car, and not caring if I went to prison either. Her husband deserved to know what she was like.

I was outside Tracey's house again. All the lights were off. I supposed they were in bed. I wondered if they had shouted at each other, had they been in turmoil too? Or had it not been confessed at their house?

Realisation was all over me, and I heard Marks words in my head " I'm leaving you" and I realised that this was really happening. The cold, tingling feeling was back, spreading all over me. Somewhere in the distance I could hear a whaling noise, and then I realised that the noise was me, I was stood under the yellow lamps, crying hysterically, almost strangled by my own sobs.

I started to run back the other way, away from the light, back towards the woods, where it would be dark and quiet.

Full confusion had set in for me by that point. I couldn't understand how I was coming home to make dinner only a few hours beforehand, and then all that I knew was shattered. I looked at my phone and it was nearly 11 at night. I knew it was late to call someone but I felt like I had to tell another person just to get all the words and the noise out of my head, the conversation I had with Mark just kept playing over and over again, stuck on repeat.

I dialled Mum.

The phone rang and rang for a long time before mum eventually picked up, answering as I would expect at that time of the night with a concerned "hello?"

"Mark is leaving me" I croaked "He has been seeing some woman called Tracey and he said that he doesn't want me anymore and that it's all over, I am losing him, I am losing everything."

I told her everything, from the kissing with Tracey, the way he didn't want the bills, this life, this time with me. The more I told her the more real it started to sound, the cold feeling was washing over me again, tingling all over my body and I felt like I couldn't breathe, as I was speaking to Mum, I was secretly hoping that as it was the middle of the night, maybe I would wake up and it was all some sort of horrendous nightmare.

At first, she was quiet, when she did speak, chose her words carefully.

"Oh, darling I don't know what to say, I bet he will wake up and feel different tomorrow, and change his mind, it does sound as if he is very, very unhappy, and you probably need to talk things through"

"But mum, you don't understand, he is not Mark, he is like someone else, he is saying things that can't be true, that he would not think. He doesn't even look like Mark, I just want the old Mark back" I cried as I sat on the pavement at the edge of the woods, stubbing my feet into the dust and grit with my worn trainers. My eyes had adapted to the dark and I could see all around me.

Mum couldn't know what I knew. She didn't see his face, how all the emotion and care had gone from him and the man who once put his arms around me and saved me from all hurt and pain, was now the one causing it, and there was nobody to save me.

Mum managed to persuade me not to hurt Tracey, or her stupid car and that I should walk home, get some sleep and try and talk to Mark in the morning.

I got back to the house and Mark was sat at the bottom of the stairs.

"I have been trying to ring you" he said quietly " I thought you had gone off down the trail and hurt yourself, even tried to kill yourself, but I couldn't find you anywhere"

My stomach did a little flip as I thought, so he does care, the cold feeling warmed slightly as I looked at him, searching for a feeling of emotion across his face, just the tiniest sign that he still loved me.

"I am glad you are safe anyway" he continued "I've moved some stuff into the spare room, and I am going to bed now"

I started to cry again, the seeming care for me had been some sort of a, horrible trick and I started to sink into the cold again, it was pulling at me, trying to drown me some more, and was back all over my body. "Please don't do this Mark" I pleaded. I was appalled at my voice, the sound of the begging and whining.

He simply replied "I am sorry Ruth"

He went up the stairs, into the spare room, and shut the door.

I sat at the bottom of the stairs and the dogs looked at me. Wondering I guess which room I would go into, and who should they follow or perhaps they were just unsettled by the evening's goings on.

After I had been in the bathroom, I got into bed beside Mark in the spare room. I knew I wasn't supposed to, I knew he was in there because he had banished himself from our marital bed, but I felt that surely if I held on, if I didn't let him go, he wouldn't actually go, I was more than prepared to show him in all my desperation that I did love him and need him.

I got in bed beside him and snuggled up close, both of us were wearing pyjamas, something we would have never normally done, so I couldn't feel the usual warmth of his skin.

He started to roll away, to his side of the bed, away from me and I couldn't seem to get close to him.

Eventually I must have dropped into a light and wine fuelled sleep, with no rest.

I dreamt that I was stood at the bottom of our garden. I looked up to the house, to the kitchen window. I could see another woman looking back at me, looking out of the window. She was washing pots in the sink and stacking them on the worktops. She was stood in my kitchen, stacking my limited edition denby plates onto my sparkly blue granite worktops. She had brown hair and appeared to be very beautiful. She looked up, and out of the window and towards me and laughed.

I woke up with a jolt.

Before I opened my eyes I knew that the world I was waking into was far removed from what I had ever known. It was broken.

Thursday 27th May 2010

I somehow managed to drive myself over to the horse's yard that morning. When I got there, I didn't really know how I had arrived there, and I had no recollection of the journey.

It was still quite cool in the morning sun, and I was wearing a jumper and still shivering, but it probably wasn't the cold, it was probably the excessive wine and lack of food. As well as my body shaking my mouth was dry and my head felt thick. When I looked around too quickly the whole world started to spin, and I struggled to stay upright unless I went very slowly. But all of these physical things would pass. I could cope with the hangover and the tiredness. But I couldn't cope with the feeling inside me, inside my soul. Like Mark had somehow reached into my body the night before and squeezed my heart so hard it had almost stopped. But somehow it was still beating, and I was still alive, but the pain in my emotions was close to making me wish I wasn't.

For the horses nothing had changed, they were still pleased to see me, munch on their breakfasts in their brightly coloured bowls and once they had finished, they went away to graze on the lush spring grass, still damp with dew.

I watched over them, looking all around the yard, at the lovely stables, made of sturdy brick and strong wood, still smelling of the recently applied creosote protection. The big generous hay barn. The large green fields with the solid stock fencing, and the trees lining one side of the field, creating a good shady spot for sweaty horses on a summer's day.

I realised that everything that was around me here would eventually be no more, I would have to move house, it was likely the horses would have to move, and this place where I had learned to come for my peace and quiet and to relax with my equine companions was likely to be no more for us.

I thought that I should drive back to our house, and talk to Mark. I needed to get him back to the old Mark, something must have gone wrong, and I was sure that once he saw me then he would change his outlook on things, that this was all just some temporary state of mind he had gone into.

But as I drove up our street, I could see his car going off in the opposite direction, towards the office where he worked. I glanced at the clock in the car, even though it was only 6.30am he must have decided to go to the office. I guessed that was easier than facing me.

I felt another chill ooze over me, there is was again, all over me trying to pull me down, almost crushing the air out of me. I had lost my opportunity. How could I make him see that this was wrong if I couldn't talk to him?

I called his mobile in desperation, I must have called it more than ten times, but he didn't answer, I imagined him sat in his green, wheeled, chair, watching the phone singing at him and vibrating along his desk, but unable to answer it. Unable to have a conversation with me, too exhausted from the barrage the night before and the feelings inside of him that had driven him to his decision.

At this point I started to feel very weak and tired, I hadn't eaten for nearly 24 hours, and I had barely slept. In the silent house I fed the pets and I got dressed for work, avoiding any mirrors to keep away reality.

I drove over to the offices where I worked. I made it half of the 30 minute journey before a song came on the radio.

"Guess she gave you things I didn't give to you" Every word of this song felt so real and was so true. It was like it was my words, being sung back to me, coming out of the radio and stinging and biting me.

By the time I stopped the car I was soaked in my tears. It had been a good decision not to wear any make-up.

As I was going up the creaky wooden stairs to the first floor, a feeling of dread started to come over me. I was going to have to try so hard to pretend that everything was OK, to manage to be strong and get through the day. As I dragged myself up the last step, I just didn't know If this was going to be possible.

I swung the reception door open. The company administrator, Elaine looked up from her typing. Concern swept over her face. "Ruth, what on earth happened" I guessed my lack of make-up, swollen eyes and pale cheeks were enough to give me away. I swallowed hard before I spoke.

"Mark has left me, he is seeing someone and he doesn't want me anymore' "

And so it began. I had to tell the same story to every person in the company, one by one. They all knew something was wrong as soon as they saw me; I couldn't hide it from anyone. My life was usually jolly, and I don't have sad tales of woe to tell, I tell stories of drunken parties and funny things that have happened with my horses. But all of a sudden I was plunged into having to explain to people what has gone wrong for me like it is an episode in a ridiculous soap drama. I had to watch each persons shocked and horrified face.

The cold feeling was all over me again and again, and the embarrassment. My perfect life was pretend. And I had an audience to add to my torment.

I sat at my desk. It was always a cluttered mess with project folders all over the place, and used coffee mugs and glasses, pots of pens, and bits of biscuits stuck in my keyboard. As I sat in my chair, I felt that unexpectedly this familiarity gave me some comfort. I made a silent deal with myself. Telling the staff had been more terrible than I could possibly imagine, so I would not even attempt to tell any of my customers.

I tried to get into my daily routine. I tried to be normal. I took some phone calls; I made some phone calls.

Elaine kept making me coffee. Somebody ordered me some breakfast. But when it arrived I could not imagine eating it. The thought of putting any food in my mouth was making me feel physically sick, I was almost retching, as I stared at the bacon sandwich, the normally appealing snack turning my stomach over and over.

The directors called me into the meeting room. I took a deep breath. I didn't know what this meeting would be about and if I could really cope with any serious conversations.

I went into the board room. It was cold in there. I sat on the edge of one of the worn blue seats. I concentrated my focus on some white fluff sticking out of a hole in the furniture next to my thigh.

The three directors are all watching me closely. It was Jane who spoke for the group.

"Ruth, we think you should go home" she was calm and measured. "We are really sorry for what has happened to you, and we are all very concerned. Stay in touch and we will see you tomorrow"

"Thank you" I whispered. Grateful tears were stinging my eyes as I stood up and exited the room, unable to provide any further communication.

Thursday 27th May 2010 part 2.

I drove back to the house, and once again, when I had arrived at my destination I had no idea how I got there and could not remember the journey. I found it remarkable how I had no memory as soon as I stopped the car.

I got into the house, and the dogs came bounding up to me. We went to the lounge and I collapsed onto the thick pile beige carpet. I sat and cried and cried until there was nothing left in me. Blubbering into Mia and Phoenix's fur, wondering if they had any concept of why?

I couldn't stop my mind wandering through all the happy times Mark and I had shared together.

The times we had sat on this very carpet together and kissed and played. We were always teasing each other ticking, pinching, and eventually taking each other's clothes off.

And now I was sat here on my own, in this reverse reality. A parallel world had literally cropped up overnight that we didn't really belong in, and I couldn't understand why Mark felt the way he did. I started to consider that maybe he was ill, and perhaps this was some sort of a bizarre mental breakdown. He didn't even look like he did before, his usually smiley face, last night it was gaunt, pale and drawn. I thought he needed my help, surely?

My phone beeped, interrupting my trail, a text from Mark "Want to meet at McDonalds and talk?" It suggested.

I started to shake, with fear and excitement. Staring at these words I could feel some hope, maybe he had reconsidered and realised we were meant to be together.

So I got up from the carpet, patted the dogs, and left the house, straight away, like a loyal little servant beckoned by her master.

We sat down together outside. It was another warm day, and the sun had encouraged people in droves. McDonald's was very busy, with cars constantly streaming along the drive through section, as I looked over and through the glass, all the other people seemed to be smiling and enjoying themselves.

I held my chocolate milk shake and Mark held his coffee. I looked at my shaking hands and glanced at his, also trembling. As I looked at his left hand, I gasped as I realised his wedding ring was gone. The cold feeling was all over me, right up my arms it went, into my body and all over my face, as a knife like feeling stabbed at my stomach and chest like it was ripping me inside and I gritted my teeth hard. Trying to be brave and strong.

"Where has your wedding ring gone" I whispered "It's in my draw at the office, I have locked it in there out of the way, I don't want to wear it anymore." So plain and sure in his response. As if I was just a nobody to him.

It felt like Mark was killing me again, just like the night before, his invisible hands inside my chest squeezing my heart.

"I can't take mine off just yet you know" was all I could mumble back to him.

"That's OK, you do what you want when you are ready, I will try and help you through this Ruth you know."

I couldn't take the pressure anymore and the tears were rolling down my face, despite me trying to fight them inside.

"Thing is Ruth, I've been talking to people at work, and I have been talking to them about how I feel, and how I need to be happy, and why I need to leave you, and I have realised that you always get what you want to make you happy, I always give you what you want to be happy, and I don't try to make myself happy, and I need to be happy, I need to feel happy."

Happy, happy, happy, what was he saying?

He looked up at me, I just stared at him, because I couldn't actually speak, the sickness, the faint feeling and the cold feeling, I was frozen to the spot in a trance.

"I was talking to Carrie and I realised that I never wanted that expensive kitchen, I never wanted the things in it, I didn't need the expensive, blue , glittery, worktops , we got them because you wanted them, I didn't want them at all, but you got carried away and I let you. Same with the rest of the house, I don't think that I ever wanted any of those things"

I sat staring, totally lost in my thoughts, because Mark had been so involved in choosing the carpets, the curtains, the kitchen fittings, never at any point would I have thought he didn't want any of this, any of these things, I desperately wanted to try and understand. But where had Mark gone? Who was this man saying these things to me?

"I don't want the house with all of the expensive rooms in it, I don't want these bills, this existence, I just need to be able to spend some time and some money on me. I am going to live at Mum and Dads for a bit whilst we start to sort this out."

It seemed that there wasn't much more for us to say to each other at that moment in time. And anyway I couldn't really speak. I was left numb. Silently we walked away from each other, and got into our separate trucks and drove away in different directions.

Afterwards I drove straight to the horse's yard and walked into the middle of the field, and sat on my pink, plastic, mounting block. It was hard not to look at every position and over analyse it. The mounting block, for example, it had been pricey, but I did need it, there was no way I could climb on to my two massive horses without it, and it was better for them too. But I wondered did Mark think I shouldn't have had it? I started to consider, this was all my fault, my neediness, my materialistic ways, had I somehow driven him to feel like this?

I sat on the mounting block for hours, not moving, not crying, not speaking. I was just staring into space. Occasionally my mare, Lazer, came wandering over to me for a fuss, her large black face rubbing against mine, and pricking me with her whiskers.

That night Mark came back to the house and collected a rucksack full of things, some clothes and some toiletries.

As he left I was standing in the kitchen, stirring the chocolate milkshake I still had from McDonalds earlier on, I couldn't eat, I couldn't drink, I couldn't even consider putting things in my mouth.

"I am sorry Ruth, I just need to be happy" he said as I followed him out of the kitchen, into the hall and to the door.

And with that the front door closed behind him, and I felt more alone than I had done in my entire life.

27th May 2010 part 3

Once Mark was gone and I was sat alone with my thoughts I started to send text messages to the closest members of our families. I was desperate for some advice, or some input from one of them that would help me to change the situation I had found myself in.

Everyone responded the same. None of them could quite get their heads around why this was happening either, they were all in shock. They never thought our journey through life together would come to an end.

My mother in law, Carol recollected that she and Patrick were the same age as Mark and I when he first started behaving differently towards her. At a similar time in their life's, he had his first of several affairs. But he always came back to her. She wondered whether Mark was going through a similar crisis, the need for other women just a temporary pull away from our relationship, and he would change his mind in time.

My sister-in-law Joanna replied that she thought the discovery around Mark and Jane and the secrecy they shared together was a symptom Mark was venturing into relationships with other ladies. She maintained this had affected me much more than I had let on at the time, and perhaps what was happening now was somehow connected. She also recalled to me how she went through the same feelings as I was experiencing when her relationship with her ex-partner was over.

My sister Kate was the most distressed. And sorry, sorry she was in Edinburgh and couldn't be with me, she wanted to help, but felt powerless so far away.

As I cried and screamed to her she tried to shush me and calm me. As we were on the phone I was sat on the landing, surrounded by my wedding photographs, the people were all looking down at me from the walls.

The happy, beautiful families all dressed in white, beige, and blue, set in the amazing Greek countryside. I looked at my favourite picture. It was Kate and I, smiling at each other, arms interlocked, in our carefully chosen dresses. Hers had been chosen to match and compliment mine. We had flowers in our hands and confetti in our hair. We looked joyous, our smiles beaming away.

And in that split second, I knew that we would never have that moment again, where she is my bridesmaid at my wedding, helping me with my hair, putting it up into careful blonde curls. Picking up the long train of my dress and putting me in the wedding car, struggling to fit in beside me and my huge dusty pink dress, laughing with each other.

I wouldn't have the moment when Dad cried as I came out of the apartment. He stood and cried at how pretty I looked and told me he was so proud of me. And we all three walked to the wedding car, and together we travelled to the winery.

There were pictures of me getting out of the car and Kate re-arranging my dress for me. Dad stroking my hair. And we walked down the stairs, and the whole family was stood at the bottom of them , cameras in hands snapping away at this, the happiest moment of our life's. Mark and I were the stars of our very own show.

But I was not there, we were not there. There was no Greek Cliffside, there was no winery. There were no happy and proud families.

There was just the landing, with me sat on the white carpet, looking at memories that weren't mine to keep anymore.

I wanted my sister here now, to hold me and give me back the strength I had lost.

The conversation with Kate over, my mind started to work overtime, considering everything that Mark had said in great detail. The fact he didn't want all of these material things, and more importantly how he had said that I was suffering from a bi-polar disorder, that he felt I was mentally ill.

Suddenly a thought was triggered. I had a healthcare cover plan with my work, which offered a free counselling service, I knew then that I should call them, they would be able to mend and repair me, resolve these discovered faults, and then Mark would want to come back.

I paced up and down the chequered patio outside, on the phone for at least an hour to a counselling service.

I spoke to a man with a Scottish accent, he had a gentle, soothing voice. He asked me if I wanted to hurt myself or kill myself even. I answered that "I just don't want to be here at the moment" it was all I could say to him to describe my feelings at the time.

When I had first started the conversation, I could hardly speak, but after a while all my words came tumbling out and I could explain things more clearly.

The man suggested that I could go for counselling, probably marriage guidance counselling would be best, maybe someone like relate. He suggested that I could go with Mark, but if he declined then I could attend on my own.

Feeling slightly better I agreed to make an appointment with my GP who would need to see me in person for the make a referral. I felt a small sliver of hope build inside myself as I ended the call.

Abandoning the waterbed

When Mark and I moved into our big house, we had made a good amount of equity on our first property. We treated ourselves and our new home to some lavish accessories we had been dreaming about.

Marks parents had a waterbed. Comfortable and quirky we had always wanted one.

We bought an enormous crib, 7 feet by 6 feet, hard side, covered with black leather all around and a large black leather headboard to match. It was excessive but we loved it. Always warm and comfortable. Obviously as the marital bed it represented a passionate place and a place where we could curl up together for a chat or just hold each other for a while. We called it our safe place.

We had decorated our bedroom with ornate wallpaper with large black flowery patterns, against a cream background, which was soft and textured like velvet and felt nice to touch. We had a large black chandelier over the bed. Our room led to an ensuite bathroom with a white and silver sparkly theme, we had decorated that ourselves too. I recall my great joy at discovering glittery paint was available.

Best of all we a walk in wardrobe, every girls dream; I could saunter in to be surrounded by all my clothes, shoes and handbags, and I even had my own little mirrored dressing area.

When Mark left I could not face the thought of a single night in the bedroom or the bed alone. It had been designed by two people for two people, and I was only one person, one person who the other no longer wanted to be with.

The bed was vast for such a small person, and I would feel lost and alone. And suddenly it didn't feel like a place I wanted to sleep. It would no longer be a place of comfort and enjoyment. It had been abandoned by Mark and it would be abandoned by me.

I moved my alarm clock and pyjamas to the spare room. It was pink and girly and had a small double bed in it. If felt safer and more familiar to me.

But the first night I got in the bed and buried myself in the thick purple duvet I felt alone. I couldn't get comfortable. Tossing and turning, sleep would not come.

I had the radio playing to try and help relax. But the song I was most afraid of hearing played "telling me, touch me, feel me, and all the time you were telling me lies" I tried to bury my head under the pillows, but I could still hear "Have you ever tried sleeping with a broken heart?" How apt. And no I couldn't sleep with a broken heart.

Mia and Phoenix were not allowed on the furniture. They had their own beds for dogs, but sensing me stirring they had gently climbed up. Mia is a sensitive dog and I really believe she knew at the time what was happening. As I had lay in the dark, tears pouring down my face, feeling sicker and sicker,

Mia had licked the salty droplets and snuggled herself next to me, pawing me gently and Phoenix curled up next to my head on the other side.

I was slowly able to find some comfort like this and I could drift off.

The spare room had become a sleeping den for the three of us.

Friday 28th May 2010

I can remember that I didn't want to open my eyes. I didn't want to wake up. I knew instinctively even before I woke that something was wrong. A sensation that as you come into consciousness from your sleep a prickle tingles all over your skin, and your mouth is dry, and your eyes are sore.

Sleep had offered me no release, and as I woke up into a reality I could not bear, I knew I wouldn't really be able to cope with the day ahead. It was just too real. Defeated before I began.

I sat on the edge of the bed in the spare room. Surrounded by the purple duvet covers and pillows, and the dogs who were also rolled up in the sheets with me. Pharaoh cat sat on the pink carpet looking up at me thoughtfully.

The house seemed so quiet with only me and the pets in it. I had never lived on my own, and spent a few rare nights alone whilst Mark was working away. But knowing that there was only going to be me in the house longer term was something I couldn't even consider at that moment in time.

I stared at the dressing table, where all my perfumes sat. They were mostly bought and chosen for me by Mark. He was very good at guessing what I liked.

The bottles lined up, one of them very long and tall, and I could remember him buying this one for me on a flight back from our holidays. I had smelled it when the flight attendant went around with the testers, said how nice it was, and the gentleman sat next to us had bought it for his wife, and I felt a little envious. But I had no need to be, he was in on a little trick with Mark, and when the in-flight dinners got passed round, mine had a wrapped bottle of perfume in it from Mark.

He was so thoughtful like that. Always treating me…..his words in my head now, always giving you what you want…..

I wriggled out of the covers and went across the landing to the office room. I switched the computer on, thinking that I may as well log onto the server at work, and check my emails for anything important.

The home email opened automatically as the computer started, it was a shared account.

Unfortunately, Mark had left this email account linked to some social networking sites, and I could see all the correspondence between him, and a girl called Claire. About things they wanted to do to each other, how they were going to meet up. She was asking him how he was. I felt hot and then cold wash all over me, one sensation after the other, angry and distraught, nauseous, the imaginary knife that lay permanently in my stomach was ripping at flesh again, trying to make its way up to my heart.

The link I followed to the site showed me her picture. She was broad, overweight, and looked very plain, not a trace of make-up and no hair style so as to speak of. He was messing around with her over me??

I stood up and looked in the mirror behind me. Things had got to change, if he could be attracted to her then I needed to make much more of an effort with myself. Loose more weight. Tidy myself up, get my hair highlighted again, buy some new clothes and re-invent myself?

But then there I was again, the tears were rolling down my face and I was a howling mess, sinking to the office floor, chocking on my tears, unable to move.

For a brief moment the anger I felt came back to me over this woman, this ugly woman who knew Mark was married from his status information on the networking sites and thought that it was OK to carry on with him anyway. I grabbed my mobile and dialled Marks.

"Mark, who the hell is Claire?" I shrieked, and I didn't wait for him to finish "She is disgusting, I can't believe you are seeing her, what is going on?"

"Oh crap, I'm sorry you have seen that, there really is nothing in it Ruth, nothing going on, she is just a friend and she has a crush on me." He seemed honest in his tone.

I knew I was supposed to stay strong, show him how tough I could be, but I lost my willpower and my emotions won.

"Take the link from our home email to your social networking sites away, NOW!" I screamed at him down the phone "I am in hell here, and I can't cope with this right now, I really can't cope with just how easily and quickly you can move on!"

I hung up, by then I was lying on the floor of the landing, the dogs were licking me, worried about all of the noise, I was in a pool of my own sweat and tears.

I dialled another number this time to my boss. "John I'm really sorry, I'm not coping very well, I can't come into the office, I need to go to the doctors and get some help" I mumbled.

"That's OK Ruth, I thought you might say that today, I was surprised that you managed to come in yesterday to be honest" he understood about martial problems and the stresses caused by them from his own experiences "Just drop us a call later if you feel like you want to come in, it might do you some good to take your mind off things that's all."

But as I hung up I knew it wouldn't, nothing would, because the life I wanted to live in wasn't there anymore for me, it felt like it had been stolen and replaced.

The next call I made was to the doctors. I said it was an emergency and I needed to see someone, and got an appointment within in a couple of hours.

I thought maybe I should make some coffee. I hadn't eaten anything for a couple of days, but I needed the caffeine, it was the only source of energy I could stomach.

I went downstairs and let the dogs out on to the garden and started to boil the kettle.

Staring into space the voices inside my head were talking. And someone was singing. I could hear our song in my head. I walked up and down the kitchen briskly and noisily clattering the tiles, the tune got sung over and over in my ears, it wouldn't stop.

"See I've always been a fighter, but without you, I give up"

I texted some of the verses to Mark, in the hope that maybe with everything those words meant to us, this would persuade him and make him realise. Maybe I could change his mind?

I was transported back in time by my memories, back to the evening of our wedding reception. After we were married abroad, we had a big party and reception back home in England. All our friends and family came; it was touching to have everyone dear to us in one place together.

We had an arch of pink and cream balloons to walk under into the main reception area, helium balloons all around the room and large pink flower arrangements on tables (which I gave to close female family afterwards as a thank you for all of their help) The room had looked beautiful that night.

I had spent some time with my sister-in-law Joanna, who was helping me plan what foods and drinks we would need to order in for the occasion, including a chocolate fountain, and a massive stand for the huge cake that mum had made and decorated.

My brother Jack was in a band and he had written some songs for us and his band performed them and afterwards there was a disco, and just about everyone embarrassed themselves throwing shapes on the dance floor, and crooning in silly squeaky voices courtesy of the helium.

We were taken home by limousine, with the bubbles still flowing, stretched out in the back like a pair of happy millionaires, surrounded by thoughtful gifts, flowers and balloons.

Mark had carried me in through the front door, we were laughing as we struggled with my enormous dress, and then he carried me all the way up the spiral staircase.

We had drunk more champagne in the spare room where the sound system was and as the DJ didn't have the first song we had wanted, once we were back home, we played it ourselves, dancing, arms around each other tightly, staring back into each other's hazel eyes.

The kettle boiled and jolted me back to reality. I wasn't in that house anymore, I was back in the kitchen, the pearls on my dress, the gold cummerbund and the love in each other's eyes faded away, as Mark replied to my text message.

"Stop this Ruth, its over'"

Once again Mark got to kill me, and take away everything that was precious to me, and meant nothing to him. I didn't understand how or why.

Later at the doctors the lady GP listened to all that I had said calmly and patiently. She handed me a questionnaire. "I need you to fill this out, and I need to know if you would like signing off work for some time?"

"It's OK, I have a week's holiday now anyway" I said, realising as I did that I wouldn't be spending it doing any of the things Mark and I had planned.

The doctor appeared to be genuinely worried about me, making notes carefully, she also said she could arrange some counselling for me. She urged me to go away and complete the forms she had given me. Weirdly she offered me drugs. She said there were drugs that would help calm me and numb me and help me sleep. But I didn't want that option and declined, feeling that I shouldn't fill my body with tablets and pills.

After I had been to the doctors I drove to the yard to see the horses. I sat on my mounting block again in the middle of the field. I didn't feel like I had the strength to do anything with either of the horses, not even to groom them, let alone ride them, but I did find some peace in my head because I was being near them. Hours must have passed whilst I sat in the sun on the mounting block, day dreaming my life away.

I headed home and took the dogs for a walk. I started to enjoy the lightheaded feeling walking the dogs, having eaten nothing for a few days. It was like a little personal battle, not eating when I was hungry to prove I was at least in control of some part of my life.

That evening I drove over to my brother and sister in laws house. Martyn was out, he had gone to Carol and Patrick's to see Mark. They were together in crisis.

Joanna opened the door to her house. "Oh my god Ruth, look at you, I swear you have lost so much weight in just a few days, you look so small and slim and tiny"

I could tell she was a bit shocked. If I was being honest, when I look in the mirror I was a bit surprised too.

Joanna had made some pizzas, but I couldn't eat anything. When I looked at the ham and cheese it didn't even look like food, nor did it smell like it, I had no appetite and even snacks that I would normally crave seemed to have no smell or flavour.

We talked about everything that had happened.

We were going over every little piece of ground.

"Ruth, can you remember when we were in Kenya, and you dropped your camera in the street, and it got a bit damaged?" Joanna asked. And I could "Well Mark shouted at you in front of all of us, and I didn't like the way he spoke to you, the way he always spoke to you, so commanding, trying to order you about and control you." I thought back, and how I never questioned it at the time.

"Thing is Ruth, you won't feel like this now, believe me you won't, I know how it feels, but I have always thought that you were a strong person, and I know you can get through this, and I think you will come off so much better at the other side, without him."

Joanna was right. I didn't believe her. I wanted to but I couldn't. I had taken on every challenge in my life with Mark at my side, since I was 17 years old, and 12 years later I could not remember how to exist alone.

She was deadly serious in her expressions, and so frank and to the point.

"There is one thing Ruth, once this has happened to you, you will fall in love again, meet somebody you want to be with, I promise you will, but you will always hold a little back for yourself, you won't give all of everything to another person like that ever again."

These are words that were so valuable and so true, and have stayed with me through everything, and I feel I can now validate them as real.

Saturday 29th May 2010

Throughout everything that happened my Mum was brilliant. She rang me all the time and came over to the house as much as she could.

Mum also recognised the need for me to talk. To go over what was spinning around in my head endlessly. She was careful to empathise with me, but also kept concern for Mark.

By the Saturday I was feeling very weak and tired. I had still eaten nothing and I was surviving on coffee and water.

When Mum arrived I was particularly contrived, I had one feeling of relief that I wasn't stuck with my own thoughts any longer, but the other was that I needed to be strong. Stay tough and battle through. I couldn't cope with seeing other people worrying about me and pitying me. I was repulsed by my own neediness. But at times I just couldn't fight the emotions. Mum helped to give me some emotional strength to build me up, her usual tendency to get upset over a difficult situation gone, and she had turned into a solid super woman.

She had also made me an enormous lasagne. I probably looked at it like it was an enemy, not really knowing what to do with it, but Mum insisted that it must be eaten. All of it.

It was a warm day again, we were both dressed in shorts and vests and set of down the trail behind the house with the dogs, I am sure they were grateful of my need to walk more than usual. The track runs several miles through woods and fields to the next village, and there was plenty of time to air our woes.

As we walked, I went over every detail, plainly, telling Mum all about what Mark had said, both in person and in text messages. I was telling her what I thought I needed to do next, like putting the house on the market, and starting divorce proceedings, and wondering which solicitors I should choose. It was if being business like about the situation I could try and distance myself.

We were marching along between the trees, chatting away and I was managing to stay upbeat.

But for me it was a cruel mind trick and all of a sudden, the cold feeling was all over me, it had started as an odd tingle in my ears, but then crept all over my body, with the sickness, the stabbing knife in my stomach, and I began to ramble.

"I always thought Mark and I would grow old together Mum, I am not yet 30 and he has put me on the shelf and now nobody will want me, I have been rejected" I heard my little voice say. I couldn't see anymore; the tears had blinded me and I had fallen on the floor into some mud.

But mum had me in her suddenly strong arms. She hauled me to my feet. And she shook me hard. She brushed off the loose, straggled, hairs that were stuck to my wet face.

"Ruth, please don't say that, there are many people who will want to be with you, you will find other men in your own time, and trust me you will not be short of offers darling"

I didn't believe her. It was not Mum that I doubted it was me. Who would put up with me? Who would tolerate my personality issues that Mark had told me about, and all of my pets and my demanding ways? Who would possibly find me interesting and exciting enough to satisfy them?

Mum held me until I had stopped crying and babbling. Encased in her arms, I don't know if anyone passed us and walked by, or if it was just us and the dogs.

When we eventually got back to the house Mum heated up some of the vegetable lasagne and chopped some salad and forced me to eat some lunch. I felt like I was 5 again, being supervised until I had eaten every last morsel.

However, whilst she was there I was safe, because someone else was in charge. I was so lucky to have her when I needed her most.

The day Carol came to see me

The following day was Monday morning.

I was sat at the horse's yard waiting for the vet to arrive. It was nothing serious, just their annual vaccinations were due. The vet was running late because there had been an emergency. I didn't mind. It was warm, and I was sat in the sun on an old plastic chair throwing the ball for the dogs. The horses were both banging impatiently at their stable doors wanting to come out.

I heard a vehicle coming down the lane so I got up to go and open the yard gates and let the vet in. But when I got there the car that was coming was Marks mums. Immediately my heart felt ready to burst with emotion.

She clambered out of the car and ran onto the yard towards me, tears pouring down her face and her arms open wide. As if by magic every tear I had in my body was springing from my eyes as I met her embrace.

We hugged for what could have been an eternity. I held her so tight, and she did me. Almost as if we were squeezing the love into each other. I smelled the familiar smell of her wash powder, mixed with the pine car air freshener she always had swinging on the rear-view mirror. I pressed my face into her sweater, hiding away from the world.

Finally, she broke away and looked at me "I just don't understand why he is doing this Ruth, I really don't" She looked into my eyes "You have everything together, all of your memories shared since you were both so young. You have achieved so much together. He won't have that with anyone else. I am just so shocked; I never ever thought this would happen. And when I speak to him things that he says don't make sense, they don't add up"

I felt an enormous sense of relief. I wasn't the only one who couldn't understand how Mark had changed, and become a different person, how some of the things he said seemed to conflict with other things that he said.

"I am so relieved that you are saying this Carol, I thought I was going mad you know?"

"No, you are not going mad. I am going to keep talking to him, at least whilst he is living with us I can try and get to the bottom of some of his feelings, see why he feels he has to change the way that he does, and explore what we can do"

Carol and I talked for at least an hour before the vet arrived. Wondering how Mark could have gone from the man he was just a couple of months ago, telling her that he loved his life, he loved being him, and seeming so happy, to this new discontented man, who needed other woman, and no bills or sense of commitments, and how un-realistic this all was.

Carol also warned me that I needed to be strong "Don't make him think you need him Ruth. Don't beg him to stay and try and keep texts and calls to a minimum, make him think you are fine without him. Men always want what they can't have, and if he thinks you are getting along fine without him then he may question some of his decisions"

As the vet arrived and Carol left she reminded me "Call me Ruth, text me, I don't care if it is the middle of the night and you need me I am here for you, I will always be here for you, and no matter what happens you will always be my daughter."

As I waved her off up the lane and turned back to the yard there were tears still in my eyes and a huge lump in my throat. I swallowed it back down hard, willing it away, along with all my weakness and fear, sinking it to my stomach where the acid would eat it up and it away.

I clipped Charlie's lead rope on to his headcollar and lead him out from the stable, preparing for his injections.

"That looked very emotional" the vet commented, raising an eyebrow, almost as if it were a question and she would like to know more.

"Yea, it's all going to be ok though'" I replied and took a sharp intake of breath "Charlie might try and get up a bit, he is a big wimp you know" I shut the chatter down, making it clear that personal discussions were closed for the day. "Ruth you silly bugger, I've already injected him when you weren't looking, now get Lazer out for me can you?"

I breathed that sharp breath back out, into a long, deep sigh of relief and smiled at the vet's attitude and what felt like such a normal conversation.

Confusing times

Sleeping had become difficult. Tossing and turning in the dark, wound up in the covers, too warm, then unravelling the covers, lying on the top of the sheets, too cold. Every time I closed my eyes people speaking, things Mark had said, things other people were saying about what Mark had said. So noisy.

I could manage to get to sleep eventually, after numerous attempts with the radio, or even the tv on downstairs, any bit of background noise helped me drop off, sounds to listen to that weren't my own thoughts.

But as soon as the morning sun crept in through the thin, pink curtains in the spare room, the cold prickly feeling would wash all over me and I would wake up in a panic. Sometimes I was dreaming, sometimes I was fully aware that I was about to wake up in a reality that I so wished was not mine.

This particular morning was like the others, starting early, me driving over to the yard to feed and check on the horses, and then setting off down the trail to walk the dogs, on a mission to walk out my inner emotional pain.

The older of the two dogs, Mia, likes to hunt. She has since she was a puppy. She is very quick and accurate.

I watched her run up a sandy bank staring into various rabbit holes. Her sleek black and tan fur was shining in the morning sun, and her huge ears like radars were picking up the smallest of sounds to decide where the bunnies might be. The end of her nose was twitching.

Phoenix came hurtling out of a large bush nosily. He is slightly smaller than her, and a yellow mustard colour. He does not possess the same hunting skills. He cannot wait quietly; patience is not his forte.

But on this occasion, he was actually chasing something, he was chasing a large adult rabbit, it was running for its life in front of him, its long legs stretched out as it tried to lengthen its stride. Poor bunny, it ran straight into Mia's path.

Seconds later she was trotting down the path with it hanging out of either side of her mouth. She was proud of herself. Phoenix barked and skipped along the side of her.

I missed Mark. It felt like a moment we should be sharing. The dogs were finally working together as a team.

I took a picture of the two of them and texted it to him.

We carried on walking down the trail.

Seconds later I got an answer back.

'Want to meet up and do something today….no pressure?'

My stomach did a little hopeful flip. We arranged that we would go to Chesterfield together for some lunch because he had to take his car to the garage.

Back at the house I went in and out of my wardrobe trying to get ready for him to pick me up, I wanted to wear things that I knew Mark liked me in. Spending ages on my hair and make-up, knowing that he didn't like me to look false. Several coats of mascara and plain lip gloss, and a white t shirt and combat trousers showed my newly svelte figure. I wanted to make an effort, putting my energy into looking my best.

When he came up the street the dogs were excited at the sound of the car exhaust, they knew who it was, and they bounced around the hallway expectantly.

When he arrived the atmosphere felt awkward. Mark looked great, his vest showing off a bit of a tan to his shoulders, his tattoos and muscles exposed, I wanted to hug him and kiss him, to feel and smell what was familiar, and what I loved. But I knew that was not allowed. Instead we stood a few feet apart to greet each other and didn't know what to say and do, how to act, like strangers after all these years. A million un-said words hung in the air space between us.

Mark and I drove over to Chesterfield. I used every single scrap of will power I had not to cry in the car, I could hear Carol's words ringing in my ears about being strong, not showing him my weak side, everyone's advise the same, don't let him see you break, let him see you strong, he won't want you when your broken.

We chatted and made small talk. We agreed to go to one of our favourite bistro's for some breakfast.

We ordered club sandwiches and chips, like when we were on our holidays. We got served some fresh coffee which smelt delicious. Whilst we were sat chatting and waiting for the food to arrive I could almost pretend that he never said he was leaving me, that we were more than friends, that we were still lovers, and we have everything. But when the food arrived the reality kicked in, and the cold feeling was all over me like a slimy grease, I couldn't escape. I started to tremble, I couldn't chew the food and swallow it, my mouth was so dry, and it wouldn't go down. How could I pretend that I was OK? It was all too much. Gritting my teeth as hard as I could I made my excuses and went to the toilets. It was so warm in the bistro and I had started to sweat. I let the cold tap trickle and washed my hands, rubbing a little onto my brow, and took some long slow steady breaths.

I went back out into the restaurant area. Mark was sitting quietly. He hadn't eaten much either. "You not hungry?" I joked and smiled at him, trying to make light of things "Not been able to eat much lately Ruth" he looked at me very seriously as he answered "No, me neither" I replied as I stared at the table, one again, unable to look at his face for fear of crying.

We paid and got out quickly, I asked to leave, I felt as if the insignificant, conversations we were having, to cover those that we should have been having were slowly suffocating us.

We dropped the car off at the garage. I didn't really understand what was going on, but some baseball capped men were sitting in Marks car with a laptop plugged in to the dash area. I tried to act as if I was interested but my mind was in other places.

Whilst they worked on the vehicle, Mark suggested that we went for a walk.

As he strode along, I tried as hard as I could not to speak; for fear that all that would come out was me pleading him to stay in our relationship.

We walked along pavements lining the industrial estate where the garage was based. It was quiet, little traffic, there were not many folk wandering.

Mark was gulping again, like he did the night he told me he was leaving , he looked like there was not enough air for him to breath, and I could see that he was wresting with some inner demons again.

I asked him what was wrong. What I wanted him to answer with was that he hated this situation, he wanted to come back, we should be together in the life that we had built, and we should grow old together. I needed him to say this. I was trembling and felt faint as I waited for him to respond, silently hoping.

"Ruth, have you ever been in a place in your life where you don't know what to do? Or what is right? If I stay then that is wrong and will make me unhappy again, like it already has, but if I go then that could be wrong too, oh, I just don't know, I need to be happy, to do what's right for me, I need to be on my own I think."

So there we were again. He had come to the house, picked me up and taken me out, just so that he could drop me down again. The cold feeling poured all over me and the knife was back in my stomach, ripping so hard and I could almost taste the bile in my throat. I was stood in the middle of this unfamiliar concrete jungle, feeling as if my whole life was falling away beneath me. Like a crevasse was opening up and I was hurtling towards it. Mark looked nervously back at me.

I asked him to take me home. I wanted to die silently away from view.

He seemed to relax a little. We drove home in silence. My mind was busy as I analysed what he had said. Taking it apart and putting it together like a jigsaw with missing pieces.

Mark hung around the house for a short while, petting the dogs, and collecting a few clothes to take back to his parents. I so wished that he would leave. Then I could stop pretending to be strong. I ached all over with the desire to just collapse and cry.

I sat with my hands folded in my lap, the soft floral cushions engulfing me in their security as the front door closed and Marks car alarm clicked.

The sound of his exhaust trailed off into the distance. I listened to it growing fainter, but wished it would be louder again, with him coming back having changed his mind, but the noise had finally gone, he wasn't coming back.

As soon as I was sure he had left the tears came. I lay on the lounge floor with the dogs around me and cried louder and louder until my lungs emptied and darkness blurred my vision.

The first counselling session

My first counselling session was booked for a week after Mark had left. The days waiting were long.

I was almost half way through my week off from work. My poor eating and sleeping habits were having an impact, so I was constantly tired and had no energy, but I could not keep still for very long, I was fidgety even when I sat.

I drove to the town where the counselling sessions were arranged. It was based in an old Edwardian style house. It was on the main road, and as I walked in through the front door I hoped nobody I knew would drive past and see me.

As if a cloud of shame hung over my head, threatening a downpour at any given moment, and the thought of being seen made this worse.

I sat in the reception area and felt like a failure. I had come to the marriage guidance counselling on my own. What sort of a sign was that?

I had asked Mark if he would join me. I had asked him several times. But his message was clear, I needed help with my anger and he didn't want to come to the sessions, because he thought the counselling service would try and trick him into staying with me.

He had stood in the kitchen the night before telling me "Ruth I am not coming to the sessions, I have been talking to people, and all they do is make you talk everything through and then try and make you stay together, even if you don't want to, even if you hate each other" the anger in his tone as he added, " and I need to be happy, and it's not fair of me to come to the sessions to try and make us stay together and give you false hope, because we aren't going to be together anymore."

So I was sat alone in the magnolia reception area, on what looked like economy deckchairs.

A small, slim, pretty lady about my age entered the room. She was dressed in leggings and a flowery top, with long brown hair in a loose plait. She was wearing lots of silver jewellery which jangled as she walked. She was quite striking. I guess I was expecting an older, rounder, plainer person and I was amused by my own preconceptions.

"Hi Ruth, shall we go upstairs?" she offered.

I followed her.

We went into a very small room up three flights of stairs. There were many more magnolia walls. This time there was an office style chair, and she gestured for me to sit.

"Well Ruth the telephone counselling service have told me a little about why you are here, but I wondered if you can explain in more details."

I told her everything. I told her that my partner of 12 years and husband of 5 years Mark had left me. I told her that I felt constantly sick, that I couldn't eat, nor sleep, that I would be arranging to see solicitors, and estate agents. I explained to the counsellor that Mark had been seeing another woman, a neighbour, this action a catalyst, which started this whole process, and now Mark has realised how he doesn't want our life anymore and he was leaving it. I described how I was still in shocked disbelief to be dealing with this situation, as was everyone else around me.

It all came pouring out, along with one of the reasons why I thought he might be leaving me. That he thinks I am always angry.

As I sat in the worn chair crying out any hydration I had left in my body the cold feeling was all over me tingling, and I felt like I couldn't breathe. The room started to spin, slowly at first then faster, the councillor's colourful top becoming a blur as the magnolia walls rushed to fold in around me.

She passed me a glass of water.

"You have done really well, Ruth, really well" a smile, leading to "thanks for telling me all about this" Her voice was calm and kind.

"I think Mark is very confused, and I think that it is more than likely you may have more to tell me in next week's sessions from things he has said and done."

The councillor set me some tasks, about trying to write down when I felt angry, was it recent or from long ago, I could go as far back as I liked. She wondered who were the people who had made me angry and what I would say to them if I could?

She mentioned that if Mark changed his mind then that would be fine, he can come for counselling on his own, or we can come together. Although she also said that she was my councillor she would be seeing me alone for my sessions. She had a likeable quality and I looked forward to seeing her again.

I got into the car. I pulled down the sun visor and looked into the mirror. My face was red and blotchy and I had mascara all over my cheeks.

I drove from town to the yard to see my horses.

I sat on the mounting block in the sun letting the hours slip away.

I don't know why but I expected that I would feel some sense of relief after the first counselling session, and as I sat on the pink plastic box there just seemed to be even more thoughts to consider. The peace and solace I so desperately sought wasn't there to be had.

The book that Kate sent

If I spent any time alone my mind would wander. I would torture myself with thoughts of holidays Mark and I had been on, places we had been, times we had enjoyed together. It was as if living in constant fantasy land was a release from the cruel reality that really existed.

At some really low moments I would go to the teak furniture in the dining room and open the left hand door. The darkness beckoning me in.

The sideboard with matching table and chairs was beautifully ornate and antique and had been a present from Marks parents.

But the left hand side cupboard should have been forbidden to me at that time. It contained all of our photographs. More importantly it included our wedding photographs.

When I was alone I would open the album. Sometimes I would get to the second page, sometimes the third. Before the tears would pour down my face and I would cry out loud, wailing in the privacy where nobody could hear my sounds. I was so desperate for something to change. I would cry until the knife turned over and over in my stomach the cold feeling all over me and sometimes I was physically sick.

The white, textured fabric album, covered with glitter, with the contents shot, designed and edited, with great care and attention by Marks Aunty. Each photograph carefully created, the blue skies and sea, and the white sandy rocks. Everyone tanned, dressed in shades of blue, beige and white. My rose pink dress was a soft dusky shade, complemented by Marks pale suit, the same worn by his brother and father. Marks Aunty had written thoughtful little comments under each photograph in silver pen. Each time I read one of the sentences it felt as if the words were jumping out and stinging me like angry wasps. It made me feel like my heart was being pulled out of my rib cage, piece by piece, with every page I turned, but for some reason I kept feeling the need to do it to myself.

But as obsessive as this pastime had become, this was by no means a healthy way for me to spend my time. I knew this. I just couldn't stop.

My mobile phone was a good distraction. If I couldn't have Mark, and it felt as if I couldn't have the memories, at least I could still have all the other people who were in them.

Of the hours I spent on the phone texting and calling people, much of it was to my family and his.

As my world was falling apart and in some ways felt as if was falling away beneath me I tried to surround myself with as much love as I could.

Because my sister was so far away in Scotland, she couldn't just drop everything and come and stay with me. I know she wanted to, but she did intense work as a physiotherapist and led a whole team of people dedicated to specialist care, and they needed her all the time. She had her flat, her boyfriend and her own life up in Edinburgh.

We spent hours on the phone. We spoke most days.

When everyone else said that it would be OK, Kate did not. When everyone else said that perhaps Mark would change his mind, Kate did not. That is not to say that she didn't worry for him, and care for his safety, she was in agreement with me and most others that he had gone through a very sudden and colossal change, but not necessarily that it was reversible.

This was a warm June day. I had all the windows and doors open, blowing a gentle breeze through the large house. The dining room had light, white linen curtains which I had drawn shut, and they billowed in the wind, tickling my shoulders as I sat at the dining room table.

I stroked the intricate silver sparkle design on the front of it, rubbing the little silver love heart buttons with my fingers. A singsong tone stopped me. Kate, almost knowing from hundreds of miles away that she needed to break my activity trail and save me from my own punishment.

"I have been doing some thinking Ruth" she said " A friend of mine went through a bad patch not that long ago, and whilst I was helping her she was given a special book by a marriage counselling company, and it really helped her, I have read it too, it's quite enlightening."

I listened carefully, if I admit slightly sceptically to begin with.

"Ruth, not everyone in the book stays together, but that's not what it is about, it's just that it helped my friend and I think it could really help you. Anyway I have already posted it."

I smiled. There is no arguing with my sister.

The day after the book arrived. It was carefully bound in brown paper and string, the presentation of a gift is as important to Kate as the gift itself. I always love opening things she has wrapped.

It came with a card wishing me well.

The kindness broke me.

I sat in the hall on the bottom step with the book in one hand and the card in the other and howled loudly. An injured animal with broken parts that couldn't be seen yet would never fully heal. The weight of my emotions gluing me to the stairs for eternity. Eventually forcing myself to lift one foot in front of the other.

I took the book on to the garden, set down a towel to lie on and began to read.

It was a collection of several stories about lovers who had gone for couples counselling. The outcomes were varied for all of them. Some remained separated. Some got back together with a new found refreshed approach to their lives in partnership.

I covered the contents in a day. I had thirst for the knowledge within the pages. A hope that they could provide sanity for my broken mind and stitches for my broken heart.

I took a leap of faith and showed the book to Mark.

I asked him again if he thought he could go for counselling with me, but he said he couldn't, for the same reasons he had stated before, he felt that they would try and make us stay together.

"That's not what happens to everyone in the book you know?" I explained to Mark "Many of them stay separated, but they all are able to deal with their issues" I tried to hide the hope in my voice that I would only ever want him to read the book and us stay together, although I suppose my motive was obvious.

"Well I'm not going Ruth, but I tell you what I will take the book and I will read it if it makes you happy?" I could hear in his voice that was his final offer.

'OK, thanks' I tried to smile. Inside I was dying; Mark had my heart in his hands again and was squeezing it. The cold feeling was all over me and I felt faint. Sometimes we know the truth but we deny ourselves turning to look right at it.

As he left the house taking the book with him he angrily slung it on to the passenger seat.

I called Kate as soon as he had left and told her what had happened.

"I just wish I could go to sleep Kate, for as many weeks, months or even years it takes for this to be over, and I can just wake up when it is all better" I whimpered "I wouldn't care that I had lost time in my life you know, I just wish I could wake up in my new existence, with this all sorted out and over and done with and I don't have to be here anymore with feeling like this."

"I know Ruth, I know, but as hard as this is and as terrible as it feels, I think you may have to go through it and experience this pain, so you can feel the true relief and pleasure when you do get to the other side."

I will always remember this advice, and I can vouch it became very true.

Kate continued to shush me quietly on the phone that night, until eventually I was able to fall into a light sleep in the spare room, the rest offering a temporary break for my tired mind and exhausted body.

The day Mark came to wash his car

It was the middle of the day and I was sunbathing. All I could find the energy for was lying in the weeds and the long grass, with the dogs and Pharaoh cat at my feet.

In my hazy dream I could hear a noise.

It was the sports exhaust on the Evo. The dogs started to jump around with excitement.

I was properly awake now and my mouth went dry. I started to tingle, prickly cold as all the hairs on my body stood on end.

I was always so desperate to see Mark, but I was never able to cope with what he said to me, even if it were answers to my own questions. Every meeting bittersweet.

Mark came around the side of the house to the back garden. Mia and Phoenix bounced at him and he stroked their heads in fondness and appreciation.

"You ok?" He said, stood there in jeans and a vest looking every bit as lovely as he always did, but I knew I couldn't get up off the sun lounger and fall into his arms " yes I guess" my voice wobbled as I answered, failing to sound nonchalant.

"I've come to wash my car and do a few bits to it" he explained

"Right, I will come and talk to you then" and I followed him, a devoted, foolish, lovesick puppy, pattering through the house to the garage.

It was almost as if we had gone back in time for those few hours. I made us drinks drinks, he washed, polished and waxed his car. It was so shiny I could see my reflection in it the grey paint. The dogs kept eagerly visiting us, bringing balls to be thrown.

Mark had the radio on in the garage and I sat in the shade on the cool floor tapping my toes to the beat.

There was a peaceful and calm atmosphere yet so many things left unsaid.

"I love this track" I told him, and to my surprise he actually went over to the stereo system and turned the sound up.

The lyrics played out "when you gonna stop breaking my heart" I shuddered and looked at Mark, he looked back at me, this moment hung in time.

"It's killing me too Ruth you know" he said quietly, I could just hear him over the music, prickly and cold all over me again, and nausea, and I felt like I couldn't breathe, like my lungs weren't taking in air.

"Then why are you doing it?" I asked him.

"Because I need to be happy Ruth, I need to find what makes me happy again" and I knew that as he said that, I was not it.

I was not the thing that could make him happy. After 12 years together and all those memories shared, it was not me.

Mark must have sensed that I was broken again. He started to get ready to leave.

He packed up all of his car cleaning equipment into a bag. All of his fancy shampoos and polishes, and his favourite buckets and some sponges.

"Where are you taking those?" I whispered.

"To Mum and Dads so I have some proper car cleaning equipment where I am living" he explained, honest, no aggression in his voice. He knelt down and looked at me, face to face as he said it. He was finalising in that statement. He didn't live here anymore and he was taking yet more of his possessions to where he did now reside.

I was desperate for him to stay just a little longer, despite how miserable what he had just said made me feel. Destroyed when he was with me and broken when we were apart, it made little difference.

"You have some letters you know" I said, trying to make them sound interesting and entice.

"OK, just pop them on the passenger seat if you like" matter of a fact in his tone.

I went back into the kitchen and got Marks pile of mail. I walked back out to the car, and opened my door, the passenger door, to put the letters there for him as he had asked.

The glove box was open. My heart sunk into my stomach. The book I had given him about the couples counselling was in the glove box, buried under a load of sweets and nuts and bolts. Only a few days had passed since he had offered to read it, but he hadn't even been curious to start. I realised that Mark had no intention of reading the book. I could never make him do something that he didn't want to. Mark didn't want to seek the answers in the stories, because he was not looking for them, he had his answers already and he didn't want us to be together.

I left the book in the glove box. I doubted that we needed to talk to each other anymore that day, I felt too tired and damaged to discuss anything else, and I went back in the house and waited until I could hear the car start up and the exhaust noise fade away into the distance.

Film Night

I was in the house alone for the evening. It was just me and my pets. It was a Saturday night.

I was with just where to put myself. It was often the case that Mark and I would have watched the TV, curling up on the sofa on a weekend night and watching a couple of films. In times gone by we would have had our baths and gotten something to eat, and sat in clean fresh pyjamas munching on treats.

But that night I was just sat in the shorts and t shirt I had been wearing when I came in from the horses yard. My clothes had patches of mud and furr on them, and my hair was straggled, escaping from the pony tail I had to try to control it in, and I had no make-up on. I didn't have the energy to go and get showered, or eat, nor the inclination.

I snuggled on the sofa with the dogs and turned the TV on, a film had just started on one channel. It was a film about a young couple, who fell in love at school, got married and had children, grew up but grew apart.

As I watched the film I was getting pulled in by the Hollywood concept. Two people battling to keep each other entertained and make time for each other and make the effort. And at the end of the film it was a glossy ending, where they get back together and live happily ever after.

It hadn't even been a great movie but it had made me think, that the characters in the film were not like Mark and I, because we wouldn't be staying together.

I looked up at the wedding photographs again on the mantel piece. The knife was twisting up inside my stomach, on its way to my heart. Wedding day memories drifted.

I could hear this faint whining noise, and all of a sudden I realised that I was at the top of the landing looking down. I was on my hands and knees struggling to breathe. The noise was me moaning. There was a hard pressing pain throughout my whole chest as if my heart had literally burst. Feeling as though I was in free fall, into the darkness, trying to put my arms out and catch myself.

I couldn't stop crying, tears blurring my vision and then everything turned to black.

Mia was licking my face. She watched me anxiously. I looked up at her. I was still on the top step, a tired, trembling heap. But at least I was conscious.

I stumbled back downstairs to the lounge and sat back down on the sofa, my legs touching the cool, soft cloth as I tried to stop shaking.

A late night news programme was on the TV now, and it had become dark outside.

My body felt heavy. Like I couldn't move from my furniture cocoon. As if what had just happened to me had taken every last little grain of energy I might have had left. I drifted to sleep with the dogs draped over me, guarding their mum, and I didn't wake until it was getting light outside.

You can never be what I want

Several days had passed. Early bed again for me. Yet, in my sleep I could hear a faint ringing. As I came to consciousness, I realised that it was the house phone. I had no idea what time it was, or who could be calling, and I ran to the office and woozily picked up the handset.

"Hello" I spoke cautiously

"Ruth its Carol" I was jolted fully out of my slumber, as my stomach did a little flip, concerned over what on earth could have happened.

'He is on his way over to your house. His blood sugars are very high and he has run out of insulin. I thought I should warn you."

"Oh gosh right"', I rubbed my face, struggling to process.

"Are you alone?" she asked "yes, just me and the pets "I answered. "That's a shame I thought it would be funny if he came back and you had a house full having a party or something" she smiled, I could hear it in her voice.

Once Carol had said that I wished that too, but I was in no fit state to throw a party.

"Don't tell him I told you Ruth, I just wanted to warn you" she said calmly.

We said goodbye. I went to sit on the end of the bed. No more sleeping for me again.

A little while later the burble of the exhaust came around the corner. I heard Marks keys in the door. The dogs went bounding off downstairs to see him.

I pulled on my dressing gown and wrapped it around myself.

"Hello, are you ok?" I asked, trying to sound breezy as I walked into the kitchen where Mark was standing.

"Yes, I'm fine are you?" he asked.

"I guess so, what's up?" I wondered if the insulin was why he was really at the house.

"I just need some insulin, you can go back to bed if you like, I won't be long."

I looked at Marks body language. He was somewhere between aggressive and upset. His shoulders were held high, poised as if ready for a fight, I couldn't work out if it was his diabetic hyper or something else was wrong.

I felt cold. Like prickly grease being poured down my neck and into my body. All my hairs on my body stood on end. I felt like I couldn't breathe. I was opening my mouth to take in air, but my lungs didn't seem to be accepting it as my chest constricted tighter and tighter.

My inner thoughts betrayed me and came bursting out of my lips before I could prevent them.

"Mark, I still don't understand why this is happening. Why do you have to leave me, why can't we be together anymore?"

He moved away from me out of the kitchen and into the dining room, visibly trying to escape me and my questions.

In the lamp light he looked down at me and I looked back up at him. Marks eyes were cold. There was no feeling in them. His pupils small dots.

"You can never be what I want Ruth" he spat angrily "you are not what I want, and you never can be."

The words seemed to come through the air out of his mouth across the room and hit me in the face, as if a force knocked me backwards, onto one of the dining chairs, and I crumpled into it. All the air went out of my body as I sighed, my vision got darker and the room started to spin around me as the knife in my stomach turned over and over again.

It is like giving up hope, hearing that you can never be what someone wants. There are no harder words to hear. Like everything is wrong with you. Physically, emotionally, he wanted none of me. Despite any vows we had taken. That was long gone.

I didn't cry, and I wasn't able to speak for a while.

"I don't want you. I don't want this house and all of these bills, the cars, the horses, the mortgage, it's been like a noose around my neck, and I just don't want it anymore." He actually seemed very angry, mad that I followed him and made him answer the questions. "I want other women I don't just want you, you are not enough for me."

I sank further back into the chair. I felt like I was watching a scene in a play from a distance.

"I wish I could leave this life behind, the bills, the material objects, I would rather go and live on a boat in Greece or something. Where there would be no bills. No laptops, no internet no complex mortgages and bills, nobody making demands on me anymore."

"But what if you missed this life Mark?" I whispered, the word's just about managing to come out.

"I wouldn't…I mean I won't, because none of these things or you can make me happy anymore."

With that statement he picked up the pack of insulin off the dining room table and put it into his shorts pocket. He patted both the dogs on their heads.

"I'm going now, sorry I woke you."

I looked up at his emotionless face, his gaunt cheeks and his cold eyes. No feeling there. No person within, like a robot. No compassion for the pain he was causing.

I heard his key in the door and his car started.

I felt so useless. I could never be what he wanted....how could that be?

I walked slowly over to the mantelpiece and picked up a picture of us together, swimming with dolphins. We were laughing.

I remembered the day well. We were on holiday in the Dominican Republic with his family. They had all decided to go on a village tour. That wasn't our scene. Mark and I had opted to go to a water park where you could split your time between playing on the flumes or snorkelling in the corals with enormous fish or paddling with sharks. I am a confident swimmer but large open water with creatures lurking can make me twitchy. Not with Mark though. Mark was an exceptional swimmer. He had been a lifeguard, and when he was swimming he looked like he was born to be in the water. When I felt nervous in the deep snorkelling pool he held my hand and smiled back at me, his grin set around his mouthpiece. He led me to the giant yellow and blue fish as we touched them together.

Later we had sat at the side of a deep salt water pool in the sea, and the trainers showed us how to feed the dolphins with little fish they had caught for them. They did tricks for us and we stroked their amazingly muscly skin.

The final task was to swim right out into the water and wait for the dolphins to come and propel you along. Waiting in the deep water I would have been scared but Mark kept me laughing and joking until our dolphin came and pulled us along through the salty water, as if we weighed nothing. We had our photograph taken at the end with the dolphin, both grinning away.

I stroked the glass and the frame, snapped back to reality. I was sat in the lounge, sat under the light of the lamp, tears pouring down my face.

I felt like Mark had killed me again. His words felt like they were stinging my body all over, right into my soul, as he once again squeezed my heart so tight I felt as if it would burst and stop. "You can never be what I want."

There would be no more sleeping for me that night.

Going back to work

Having had a week's holiday I dreaded going back to work.

Life in a busy office looking after demanding clients in IT world was going to be difficult for someone whose world was falling apart.

Following Marks cruel visit, I had lay awake the night before listening to the voices in my head chattering away with their nonsense, my stomach swilling around and around. How on earth was I going to survive?

I was going to need to take regular breaks. Possibly go out every lunch time make sure that I got away from the office and the people in it. My bosses and colleagues not normally the type of people who are tolerant of emotions, I had been shown little compassion when I had suffered any loss before and I did not expect this time to be any different.

The difference being this time that I questioned if I would actually cope.

As I walked slowly up the stairs towards the first floor office the cold feeling was all over me sending shivers up and down my body and my mouth was dry, like it was full of putty or something sticky that might actually stop me from being able to speak. By the time I opened the office door my breathing was so heavy and all I could hear was my own heart pounding in my ears. I had never felt so vulnerable in my whole life.

"Hi Ruth, you look like you have lost some weight" Elaine stated as I opened the door.

"Thanks" I replied and walked quietly past, with my head down.

"Hi Ruth, thank god you are back, your clients have been playing up and I need you to help me with a load of new projects that have come in" stated Peter, the Sales Director.

I sat in my chair and glanced at James, my friend in our team and he smiled warmly.

Because everyone was acting as if nothing had happened I thought I may actually get through the first day by pretending the same thing myself. It was just eight and a half hours, if I could manage to trick myself that this was my normal life then maybe this would actually be achievable.

This tactic worked for the first few days, and I pulled it off.

On the way to work in the mornings I gritted my teeth if any love songs come onto the radio, or I changed to some upbeat house or rave music on a CD. I got myself in to the zone. I enjoyed the barrage of challenges from clients who needed to spend more money to make their IT systems more robust. I welcomed the heated debates with colleagues, those trivial and superficial problems that the awkward idiots that I worked with had come up with, they made a good job of giving me a somewhat normal existence.

On the way home I tried to call mum or Kate or Carol. Anything so I could have a discussion with someone, and avoid the radio, and any mellow tracks which may cause emotions to return.

Then when I got home I would rush inside, and fall apart. I would curl up at the bottom of the stairs in the hallway, whist the tears poured down my face, and the dogs would lick them, and Pharaoh cat would rub herself around my legs. Some days I was too exhausted to cry.

By the end of the first week, having about managed to get through, I was on the phone to a client, an office worker calling in from one of the sites the company I worked for managed; she had some sort of an issue I am trying to help her resolve.

"So how are you anyway Ruth? You don't really sound your normal self?" Oh no, I gulped and swallowed. My act has been foiled.

"Erm, I have been having a bit of a rough time " I looked around the office to see if anyone was listening in to my conversation, searching around the room nervously I realised that I was in there alone, and it was safe.

"Me too, I spilt up with my husband you know, I don't know if I want to be with him anymore, he doesn't do anything for me , he never takes me out, never spoils me it's as if he is a different man." I pictured her at the other end of the phone telling me this. She was small and blonde, curvy and pretty, like a slightly older version of me, and I had liked her the first time we met.

"Gosh , that is very similar to me, my husband came home one night about two weeks ago, and said that he was leaving me, and I am not what he wants anymore, and he doesn't seem to know what he wants anymore, but he knows it's not me" I muttered quietly.

"Ruth, you have to go to this special website I have always used, it's a prediction of what is going to happen based on your star sign and trust me this woman is never wrong."

After that part of the conversation, I had gone back to helping her with the computer problem, and after putting her through to the engineering team I put aside my sceptical feelings towards horoscopes and I went onto the internet and put into the search bar the address she had given me and started to read my prediction for the week.

It was shocking, it stated that I would have had one of the biggest trauma's of my life and I would be in turmoil. But the end of the week would either see a new beginning for me and the one that I loved, or a waterfall of tears and the end for good.

I read it and re-read it. I showed it to James. There were tears in my eyes and my stable work persona vanished, and I was back to the vulnerable person, my emotions had found me.

"Try not to read too much into it Ruth, its fascinating and very clever, yes. But I don't think it is doing you any good reading this sort of stuff at the moment." James was trying to pull me away from the emotional pit I was falling into.

But this phone call had become the start of another unhealthy obsession. From then on when I was at the office I would spend every spare moment researching my horoscope. I would go onto about five sites a day and put together what they all said and made notes in the pad on my desk.

These predictions had given me some sort of hope that I could look into the future and see something positive, the delusion that I could see Mark and I back together.

After I checked out the horoscopes page I had then sat back at my desk and gazed out of the window. I had a view of an open lake with swans and ducks floating around, trees and sunshine. But all I could think about was why had Mark has left me? I was unable to think about my clients new projects. The things that Peter had asked me to look into and start working on. They were no longer interesting to me. All that was interesting was how I could make Mark see that he was making a terrible mistake, and that we should be together.

All of a sudden it hit me. All along! He was having some sort of a mental breakdown. And the breakdown had made him think that he didn't want to be with me anymore.

I went back onto the internet again, and I searched for 'mental breakdown ruins marriage' and 'early midlife crisis ends marriage'.

I found lots of really useful information, people noting experiences similar to mine and that people having a breakdown or a crisis will often look to those nearest and find their faults, in favour of looking at their own faults and issues and dealing with them. I thought of all of the negative things Mark had been saying to me and about me, and yes, this made sense.

The article also looked into running away tactics, like the person who is having the breakdown feels so bad and so guilty about the mess that they have made of their lives that they don't want to drag others who they love into their mess, so by leaving them they are no longer exposed to it. This also made sense.

I read page after page and it all started to fall into play. I wondered, could I explain this to Mark?

I cut and pasted all of this information I had found and started emailing it to my friends and family too, then surely they would see that this was what the issue was, I hadn't gone mad after all ,Mark had and we just needed to help him.

And that was how my days at work continued. Half of the time being the office enslaved version of myself, going to client meetings, sitting with the directors and taking instructions, talking to colleagues and liaising with the engineering teams, putting plans together. Doing all of the normal things that I did. This was what I needed.

But then the other half I would crave time alone in the office when I didn't feel like I was being watched. Time to check my horoscopes, and research my problems.

This was by no means a healthy existence, but I was at least getting by.

Anthony

Having had a very busy and unpleasantly hot day at the office I had driven straight from work to the horses yard, fed both horses and driven home.

This wasn't unusual for me, my lifestyle has always been an active one, although in an attempt to keep the voices in my head from talking constantly I found I was seeking further distractions than ever before.

In the car the seat stuck to my thighs, and small strands of my hair had wound around my ears and neck, attracted to my sweaty skin. Pulling onto the drive and yanking the handbrake on I was in a rush to get out of the car. I was met by a further wave of heat when I opened the truck doors, a warm wind blowing around causing dust to stick to my bare arms and legs.

I ran into the house, breathing a sigh of relief, as the dogs bounced around me licking my salty skin.

I then ran up the cream, plush stairs, kicking off my shoes, feeling the soft carpet on my toes, throwing off hot and sweaty work attire, pleased to be swapping it for something more comfortable.

In my wardrobe I chose a pair of shorts and a vest, enjoying the thought that I would be feeling cooler.

I grabbed the dogs leads and together we set off down the trail.

Mia and Phoenix kept veering off into the field, which were filled with tall crops, excellent for canine hide and seek. They would disappear from view for moments at a time, and then leap up from out of the green wheat sea they were playing in, their ears flapping before they were gone again. My mobile phone started to ring.

It was a number I thought I recognised but couldn't be sure. I answered it with a cautious " hello?"

"Hi Ruth, its Anthony. I have been speaking to my receptionist and she told me some of what you have been going through. I just wanted to say I am very sorry. And I am here for you if you need me."

Wow, good news really didn't travel as fast as bad.

"Thank you" I stammered. My mind drifting. Anthony was the managing director and owner at one of my main client offices.

"Ruth, it sounds as though Mark has done something irreversibly shocking and stupid, but his loss in turn will be your gain. I have been in the place that you are in now, granted it was many years ago, but I know how it feels, and I know that you are going to be just fine."

I could hear the warmth in his voice. I had grown fond of Anthony and our chats. He was a lovely man with a boyish charm to his middle aged looks. He had a big laugh, and his rounded face was always smiling. It felt comforting to speak to him.

"I'm just shocked Anthony, I never thought this would happen to me you know, it's the sort of thing that always happens to other people, other people tell you these stories, and then it happens to you, and all of a sudden I have been living a lie, and the love, and the marriage it's not real anymore." My voice trailed off into a whisper. I had walked off the trail into a large corn field. The crop was all around me and felt prickly where I wasn't clothed. The sun was beating down on me, and there I was telling my deepest fears to a man I hardly knew.

"Ruth, there is only time that will make this easier for you, but I promise it will. You are a strong woman, I can see it in you, and you are very beautiful, you will have men falling at your feet when you want them and you are ready. I have to go now but I will call you again later, or text you if you like?" He sounded so sincere

"Thanks Anthony."

I hung up. I felt crushed. I didn't want men falling at my feet. I wanted Mark. How could I be with any other men? Touch their lips? Share intimate moments with them. How could I even entertain the thoughts of someone touching me like that? Just the notion made me feel sick. I wanted what I knew and what I loved I just wanted Mark. Time to retreat to a safe place.

Realising where I was I gathered the dogs and started to walk briskly back towards the house.

Once safely back home I locked all the doors, and drew the curtains, the communication to the outside world that I was safe in my den, where nobody could talk to me anymore, or force me into communication.

I sat on the sofa, staring into space. My mind wandering again.

I had a secret from Mark. From everyone.

A few months before Mark left me I had gone to Anthony's offices on a client account visit. Knowing that I was going to be seeing Anthony alone, I had emailed him in advance and asked him what he would like for lunch.

We had made a picnic area in his office and filled ourselves with chicken tikka sandwiches, crisps and chocolate Easter bunnies.

I was very comfortable with Anthony, even though I hadn't known him long, he had a way about him that made me feel trusting, and we talked about everything from when his wife left him, to when he started his own firm, to how I met Mark, and about horse riding. I found his tales of rides he had been on captivating. He spoke fondly of his favourite mare. Common ground.

When we got down to business I had reminded Anthony that his company needed to make some serious investments in the IT equipment.

He had joked with me, grinning away and jovial "Well Ruth, you see game for a laugh, what do you want to do for me to make sure I put pen to paper."

Feeling slightly flustered I wasn't sure what he meant at first, but then I had cottoned on to his flirtations.

As Anthony's suite was away from the main office, and the view from all the windows backed onto empty fields we could get up to pretty much anything I had supposed.

"You can dare me" I challenged him and stood up from his desk. Empowered by my shiny heels and pencil skirt, I leaned over him and fluttered my lashes...."what do you dare me to do, and I will do it, so long as I walk out of your offices with those papers signed."

He had laughed and smiled that cheeky boyish grin again. "Go behind that screen in the corner and take off your top and come out and show me what colour bra you are wearing."

I smiled at him as I walked past his desk, where he was sat with his hands folded in his lap, almost like a naughty school boy. The expression all over his face doubted me; that I would complete this task, this just made me know I couldn't back down from the challenge.

I walked to the back of his room, ducked behind the screens and took of my flowery blouse. I smirked to myself as I took off my bra as well, this would be funny to see the look on his face. My heart had been beating away so hard in my chest I expected to see it vibrating away before me, as I had marched up from behind him, and stood in front of him with my breasts on display.

Anthony looked up a little panicked and surprised, but his face broke into a warm smile. He stared at me for what felt like an age.

"I could come back behind the screen with you if you liked Ruth?" he asked. "I know what you would like" his voice was quietly seductive and sincere. I believed in what he was saying.

I had looked back at him and thought about it, really thought about the possibility of what we could get up to in the back of his office behind the screens, and I was sure it would feel good. The desire on his face was enough, and I could hear my heart beating in my ears as my stomach did little flips.

But within seconds I had snapped back to reality and knew I could not do it. I couldn't be disloyal to Mark. It was exciting but it was a pure fantasy.

So at the time I had gone back behind the screen alone, dressed myself and Anthony has signed off my sales orders. And I had driven away, satisfied but curious, and had not uttered a word to anyone about it. As I had left his offices Anthony had said to me "your husband is a very lucky man to have you Ruth" and smiled.

Suddenly I was back in the lounge on the sofa, my daydream was over.

My husband wasn't lucky to have me, he felt trapped, and bored and had left me, for a split second I almost regretted I hadn't taken things further.

But as I sat quietly in the dark, over analysing about it my skin started to crawl at the real idea of being intimate with anyone other than Mark.

I managed to peel myself off the sofa, where I had become almost glued, both by the humid weather and my own day dreams. My stomach growled in anger.

I went to make some food, fighting with my Pharaoh cat as she tried to steal the tuna out of the tin as I drained it down the sink.

Having had some tea I realised how late it had gotten while I had been day dreaming my life away again. It was dark outside as I peeped beyond the curtains.

I went into what had been mine and Marks old bedroom and then into the en-suite for a shower.

Afterwards I wrapped one of the soft white towels around myself and sat on the edge of the spare bed, in the room that I have now taken as my own. I glanced at my phone.

I had 5 missed calls. They were all from Anthony. I didn't want to talk to him at gone 10pm at night, I just wanted to sleep my thoughts away and get a break from the voices in my head. It started to ring again. I looked at the screen and dumped the call.

He sent me a message. "Said I would call you later, hope you are OK, talk tomorrow."

I felt angry. I just wanted to be left alone. I didn't want the flirtation or the flattery. It was making me feel sick and guilty. Appalled that I considered being with anyone other than Mark. I turned off my phone and tried to settle for the night.

The following day I had gone out of the office on my lunch break and was driving around town. I wanted to listen to the music in my car and call and text people. Sometimes I made notes on how I was feeling. Reading them back later they were ramblings and scrawls, often illegible.

Whilst I was out my phone rang. I could see it was Anthony's number. I dumped the call.

He sent me a message "Ruth I am sorry if I have done or said something to upset you but I really need to speak to you."

On seeing this I started to worry. What if it was a wholly business related matter and he needed to discuss a problem with his account, or some equipment I had sold him, and if I ignored the calls would he call the office and would I be reprimanded for ignoring him?

I dialled back.

"Hello stranger" his voice sounded calm.

"I'm sorry Anthony I just wasn't in the mood for talking last night" I apologised.

"I know, I could tell" I could hear the smile in his soft and kind voice again.

"Look Ruth I know you probably don't want to speak to an old fart like me, and I am sorry if I have upset you. I promise I won't pester you anymore, but if and when you are ready it would be lovely to see you and go out together somewhere."

I didn't know what to say, so I stayed quiet for a moment.

"Anyway that's not really why I called, I called to say that I have a recommendation for you, it's for a senior partner at a law firm in Nottingham, I thought you may want to speak to her about divorce."

"Wow, OK, thanks" I still didn't really know how to respond.

"They are good Ruth, they are really good. Do yourself a favour, just call them, tell them I said to call, get them to open a file on your case, you don't have to do anything more with it at this stage if you don't wish to. One thing is for sure Ruth, if this gets ugly and you end up in court you will want to use these people. And the other side will lose."

After we said our goodbyes I called the solicitors and made an appointment.

Then I sat in the car for a moment in stunned silence. It was real. I was really going to see solicitors, and I was really going to get a divorce.

The day we went for a sandwich

I noticed that increasingly, Mark could not seem to stay away from the house. He had promised that he needed to be alone, to be happy, and to find himself, but he just kept coming back. His actions speaking to me louder than his words.

Each time I saw him I would ache inside, wishing that we were going to get back together, and each time we spoke I asked him the same questions, the answers would always hurt me, and it felt like he got to kill me again and again. I got weaker with each rejection.

The day ahead would be no exception. It was Saturday. Again it was a boiling hot day. I had been fighting with weeds in the massive garden in the morning sun. The garden had become a complex jungle, and I was struggling to manage it alone.

Having cut some plants down and generally tidied up a bit, I had admitted defeat as the sun intensified, and got out one of the comfy folding chairs, battling dust and spiders webs at the back of the garden shed.

I had then stripped off down to my bikini and looked down at myself as I laid out on the chair. Not bad really, I was losing weight fast, and whereas normally I would be a little anxious sunbathing, I actually felt quite proud. Exhausted from the gardening and the upheaval of my own emotions I drifted off.

Mark and I are back at our first house. We are drunk. It is late at night or very early in the morning. He is kissing my neck and taking off my clothes. He gently pushes me to the floor. I am lying on soft carpet but I cant move my arms. They are tied behind my back with the sleeves of the removed cardigan. My cuffs knotted around the wrought iron of the spiral stairs. I am going nowhere. I look up into Marks eyes and smile. I trust him completely. I feel safe like this.

I was jolted awake by the sound of Marks exhaust coming down the street. I didnt feel safe anymore and I no longer trusted him. A sticky sweat covered my body as I lay in the chair listening to the engine stopping outside the house and I heard the front door open.

He walked down the garden and the dogs and the cat made a fuss of him. I didn't know what to say, I was afraid of what I might ask him and how in turn he would answer.

"Want to go for a drive?" he asked, speaking first "Yes, I will just go and get changed" I said as I walked swiftly past him to go into the house. I caught him looking at me as I went by. I prayed that deep down he wanted me again how he used to, that he looked at me and had changed his mind. But he said nothing.

In the car we were avoiding potentially difficult conversations that might cause one or both of us to become upset. We were instead saying what we had been up to, friends we had seen, how our parents were. This of course did give us plenty to talk about, as normally we would have seen these people together, so it was odd that we were socialising apart. I tried to casually mention to Mark that my Mum had asked how he was and that she was concerned for him, how he had been, and he was welcome to go and see her and talk to her. This suggestion seemed to anger him, I didn't know why, all of my family had been genuinely concerned for him , he had been behaving so out of character. And whilst I had been calling and texting his family all of the time, he has ignored mine.

We called in at a shop and chose some sandwiches and fresh fruit boxes, and once back home we had started unwrapping them on the garden, both of us eating slowly and carefully. Encompassed by this new, strange territory.

My body might have been sat on the garden but my mind was wondering elsewhere. I was thinking about Mark's relationship with other women, and I felt an overriding urge to ask him questions, possibly because I hoped he would answer that these flings and associations ,meant nothing to him, and that I was really the only one he wanted, or maybe I just had a self destruct setting within myself when I had been with him for a length of time.

"So have you been seeing Tracey then?" I asked him, my voice sounding calm and measured. " Yes, I have been texting her and met up with her a few times" he paused for a moment and glanced at me before continuing "she says that it must be very hard for you" I gulped on my sandwich, as it started to become stuck in my throat " I don't think she really gives a shit to be honest Mark" I could hear my voice coming out of my mouth but it sounded a million miles away. He carried on regardless "I have been talking to her about all kinds of things, we are both very un-happy in our lives, and we both need to change things to make us happy." He looked at me, cautiously, again "She has a horse you know, its 17HH she does dressage with him" I almost couldn't believe it, having moaned about how much time I spent with the horses, Mark had actually taken up with someone who also had a horse. Laughable. "I have told her all about Lazer, and Charlie, and I have told her all about the problems that you have had with Lazer, she says that you just need to take control of her, that you need to stop treating her like a baby, show her who is boss."

Suddenly I had more hate for that woman than I had ever felt before in my whole life, towards anybody. She was not content with stealing my husband she had decided to start criticising my relationship with my horses, something so personal to me, something that mattered to me so much.

My skin pickled and all my hairs stood on end. Invisible hands reached inside my chest and got my heart in their grip, ripping and shredding the flesh around them. Squeezing so tight, I thought it was going to burst and I could barely draw a breath.

My mind I was saying "who the hell is she to judge me, or what I do, it's up to me how I train my horse, she probably beats the shit out of hers, and I know that's not the way, I just haven't found the answer to resolve my differences with my girl yet" but I was screaming these words inside my own head.

I choked momentarily. Mark looked back at me horrified.

When I finally found the strength to respond literally all that came out was a subdued "yes she is probably right."

Loathing my weakness I got out of the heat on the garden and went into the kitchen, the cold feeling tingling all over me. Glad I could still feel my heart beating, I poured a glass of water.

Mark followed me into the kitchen, swinging his weight so he was sat on the worktop. I looked at his hands, his wedding ring still missing.

He saw me looking.

"Mum has it, it's in a safe place" He said

"Do you mind if I still wear mine?" I whispered, although it seemed silly to be asking permission "Only I was always so proud to wear it. This is a lovely ring, they are two lovely rings, and we chose them together, I was always so proud to wear this ring, so pleased to be married, so honoured to be married to you. But I know yours has been like a life sentence?" I looked up at him, my voice trailing away to nowhere as I spoke and hot tears rolled down my cheeks, and dripped onto the cold tiles, making little splashing noises.

It was quiet for a moment, no noise at all. Then Mark answered "Yes, it did feel like that. I just can't be who you need be to do be any more you know Ruth. I just can't be that person; I can't give you what you want."

I had no reply, no strength left for anything else.

Mark stroked the dogs and picked Pharoah cat up for a cuddle, I knew he was getting ready to leave.

"It aint over to till the fat lady sings you know." He said to me as he left the house.

But even with that last, puzzling, parting shot, all that he had said in the last half an hour had broken me again, and I had no idea what he meant. All I could do was lay on the kitchen floor, with the raw emotional wounds he had created, as they bled inside of me, ebbing away my energy. On the cold tiles, crying and screaming into Mia's fur until no more sound would come out.

The day Kathryn and George came

Some of my friends were a true tower of strength to me when I was in need. Some were useless. It was surprising to me who fell into which category.

It seems a sad fact that unless you have had a personal experience with the loss of a long term relationship, you don't seem to be equipped to help others deal with it.

One ought not to judge, but I never forgave some people for their shortcomings.

Of the towers of strength, Kathryn was one of them. Having had her own marriage collapse on her 8 months before mine she knew only too well what I was going through, the hours of endless questions I would sit and ask myself, the way I believed it was all my fault, she had been there.

Kathryn and I met years ago when we had been neighbours. We ended up living across the street from each other when we moved into our first homes. Mark was also good friends with her husband at the time. We socialised together as a four and had many nights out and in, usually alcohol fuelled and always hilarious.

It was a Sunday afternoon and Kathryn had come over to my house with her son George. He was perfect in every way, not yet 18 months old and already walking and talking and very robust, he was a lovely pudgy little boy. The other thing I loved about him was he had no fear dogs so as we went wandering off down the trail behind the house I didn't need to worry about my canine friends bouncing around him as he stumbled along down the path.

"Ruth, I don't know what to say, Mark has been in touch" she appeared frantic and I had a feeling I wouldn't like the sound of what was coming. "What does he say?" I asked, hopeful that it was forgiveness.

"He text me last night that he just wants to make mad passionate love" I stopped in the middle of the track, unable to hide my shock, as Kathryn continued " That he wants to have dirty sex, and do dirty things" I still couldn't quite believe what I was hearing "oh my god" I responded almost laughing, but it was hysteria, not amusement " I told him that this is something he should be talking to his wife about, not me" Kathryn went on " I am sorry Ruth, I didn't want to tell you." I could tell that there was more. I daren't ask what else has been said between them, on the one side so jealous that he could share these things with Kathryn, and on the other side horrified and embarrassed for my friend.

Whilst we continued walking Kathryn warned me about the amount of time that Mark had been spending with her ex-husband, and how he might not be a good influence, she prepared me for more partying and women, and felt that as a result of this Mark may be more hostile and horrible towards me.

By the time we had pondered over these things we had ended up outside my local pub. I saw this as a clever move from Kathryn to get me to eat, but in the warm sun it felt nice to sit at a table under a tree and get lunch. A waitress brought some water for the dogs as they stretched out, panting in the shade. Kathryn and I fed small amounts of our baked potatoes to George.

I could hear a noise in the distance. Kathryn studied me, anxiously. We both knew the sound as it got louder and louder. It was the exhaust on Marks car. The car went sailing past the pub.

'Ignore him Ruth, eat your lunch and drink your shandy!' Kathryn was firm with me and grabbed my hand next to hers. Slowly though, the prickles of the cold feeling were growing all over me, ready to spoil the mood.

I knew then that he was only a few streets away at our house.

"He was very nice to me yesterday you know" I told Kathryn.

Or was I telling myself? The day before hadn't exactly done me any good.

After we had finished our lunches, we started to walk back up the streets towards the house. I was walking faster; Kathryn and George were going slower. We both knew the same thing.

"You know he might be in a funny mood Ruth, he was out with the lads last night."

I didn't care. I just needed to see him again.

As we walked along the street we had to pass Tracey's house. She was at the top of her long sweeping drive, with a bucket of soapy water in her hand, washing her car. She was wearing a bikini and a pair of hot pants. I wondered if she knew who I was. 'Who the hell stands outside their house and washes their car in a bikini on the middle of the street' Kathryn laughed, just loud enough for Tracey to hear. I was so grateful to my friend, for saying what I didn't have the strength to. We walked on another two doors.

Marks car came hurtling around the corner.

He pulled in to the pavement where we were stood.

"You both OK then?" he swaggered. He was speaking as if he had just met us on night out. Confident and nonchalant. I looked over his shoulder, and onto the back seat. It was covered with his clothes. Pretty much all of his wardrobe appeared to be in the back of his car. Loads of other items littered the passenger seat and passenger footwell. Toiletries, phone chargers, laptops.

My heart sank, feeling like it had dropped out on to the pavement, I started to shake. He was not coming back to see me. He was coming back to leave properly, and of course to kill me again. As I stood on the curb, almost outside the whores house with the cold feeling all over me and the knife in my stomach I could hardly breathe. Like Marks hands were in my chest again, squeezing my heart with his actions. And all of this with an audience. How could he embarrass me like this in front of Tracey? I wondered if she felt victorious or disgusted, I silently preyed neither, that she hadn't noticed what was just within sight and probably within ear shot too.

Kathryn walked away slightly down the street with George so we could talk, she knew to give us the space.

The dogs sat quietly on the pavement beside me. Confused by Marks behaviour, they had picked their side.

"I don't understand why this is happening" I whimpered quietly. "I said that I was leaving you Ruth, and I am, I have taken most of what I need, so I don't keep having to come back here anymore, I know it's not good for you" I couldn't decide what was worse, that he kept coming back and killing me, or that I would never see him at all.

Nothing else to say, he fired up with ignition and he drove away.

Kathryn held me upright and walked me back to the house, making sure we had George and both dogs.

She sat me down ay my dining room table and got me a glass of water and put her arms around me. I had no cry in me . I just sat numb and in shock.

"I need to go now Ruth" she said softly "Are you going to be ok? I am going to meet someone, perhaps I should take you with me?" Kathryn was concerned. I answered in a very small voice, from a faraway place "I am going to be OK yes."

But as Kathryn and George left and drove away we both knew the truth. She would have been able to see, written on my facial expression, my hunched shoulders and my weak legs, and I of course knew I was lying to her, and to myself. I was not OK. And as I shut all the doors and made sure they were locked, I fell to the floor once again, doubting that I would ever be OK again.

The day at the animal feed shop

Another week at work passed as a blur. The weekend returned. I lay in bed listening to the voices in my head talking their rubbish. I watched the silver hands of the clock turn, awake for hours, 9am couldn't come soon enough.

I needed several bags of horse feed, and going early would hopefully mean I was likely to miss the usual hustle and bustle.

I realised when I parked up and walked in I was wrong. Michael who owned the shop was already busy with a customer, so I hung around a while looking through the notice board and waiting quietly in the corner.

I watched a spider spinning its web in the dusty window. The feed shop was small but it was like an Aladdin's cave, packed from top to bottom with every type of animal feed and supplement. Cleaning windows wasn't high on any of the employees agenda's, although, this was good news for the spider I was watching, and I was glad of him, in case someone I knew came in to the shop and wanted to talk to me. I had become fearful of conversations. I was afraid of unpredictable and tearful outbursts, which constantly threatened to embarrass me.

After the lady Michael was helping had gone, he came straight back in to the shop and turned to me.

"Ruth, forgive me for being rude, are you ok, you look very pale and have you lost some weight?" This question wouldn't be OK from just any shop keeper, but I saw Michael pretty much every week and it would have seemed uncaring if he hadn't noticed in reality. But as he asked the question a cold shiver began pouring its way down my neck, my mouth went dry and tears were building.

"Mark has left me Michael. He was seeing another woman, he has realised that he needs some time on his own, and he doesn't want to be with me anymore."

I was as honest as I could be, trying to keep it brief.

"Did you see this coming? I mean you always seems such a happy couple, him always coming in here with you and helping you with your horses, I feel so bad for you, and I apologise if I am prying."

He said the same as everyone. Shocked. Couldn't understand why. Everyone thought we were so happy. I was getting accustomed to this response.

"I had no idea it was going to happen at all, at the moment I am just trying to get by a day at a time. We have been together since we were at school; I guess I'm not very good at being on my own just yet" I spoke to him truthfully.

'Ruth, I am so sorry if you didn't want to talk about it, it's just obvious that you aren't yourself that's all." He was quiet and calm, and although I felt terrible, it wasn't because of him.

"It's OK Michael, I know."

"There is one thing though. A very similar thing happened to my daughter. I think in fact she would have been about your age. Her husband came home and said that he didn't want to be with her anymore, and they had been together a very long time and since they were at school. She was devastated, we couldn't do anything for her, it was awful. Me and her mother had to lend her money to help her buy her own little house at the time I seem to think" I appreciated Michael's story, I felt more normal when other people told me similar things had happened to them.

"Then what happened in the end Michael, is she OK now?"

"Well, this is the thing. After some time of being separated they started to talk again, then they started to go out on dates. Then her husband realised that he had made a terrible mistake and they were meant to be together. They moved back into their house and it was all OK. They have just had their first baby." Michael was beaming as he was telling me this part of the story.

"Oh wow, so it did all come good" I smiled back at him politely, he was giving me a little ray of hope.

"Yes Ruth, it did, I am not saying that's what happens to everyone in that situation. But it was the answer for them, so just hang on in there."

Michael put the last of the bags of feed on to the back seat of my car. We had been having this conversation whilst I had been ordering and paying, and loading into the truck. Michael hugged me.

"Look after yourself Ruth. I mean it." He waved as I shut the truck door and clambered into my seat.

Back at the yard, I had to sit on the mounting block in the middle of the field and stare into space for longer than usual.

I was fantasising that I would get the same conclusion as Michael's daughter.

The first time I went to the solicitors

I had little idea what to expect as I drove into the city.

The solicitors offices were in a largely pedestrianized area, so having parked the car I walked the remainder of the journey. Based in a very old building, which at the time to me looked like a restaurant, with little windows facing out on to the street, and swing boards blowing in the breeze.

I announced to the receptionist who I was and she got me seated in the reception area on the expensive looking comfy sofas and brought me freshly brewed coffee.

My chosen solicitor came to collect me. She was tall and serious looking.

In her offices she listened carefully to all that I said, nodding and taking notes.

She sympathetically handed me tissues at intervals, but she didn't bathe me in compassion, and it was refreshing. I liked her business-like approach to my situation, for the first time I was able to discuss it as if it is not happening to me. She offered helpful advice.

"You might want to think about your standard of living Ruth. "she said "for instance, you could argue that you are accustomed to a certain standard of living, with Mark as the higher earner and you will therefore be worse off, and he could compensate you by taking less of a percentage of the equity in the property, that would be quite normal."

I was surprised. It had never occurred to me to ask for more than 50%.

"If you also want to make sure that there will be no financial issues in the future, when you are already separated, you will need to go for a clean break, and have a legal agreement set out. As a part of this it will be important that you document who is having what of your largest assets, for example vehicles, large furniture, electrical goods, and also, who is responsible for paying off any debts in their name." She went on "You will also need to consider if Mark has a pension?"

I knew that he did not, whereas I did, and I also thought it may be worth something.

Sarah suggested that I considered a bargain, that we would exclude each other from any future pension right or inheritance rights. This seemed fair. Mark would stand to be a wealthy man when he finally inherited his grandparents and then his own parent's estates, I knew this from property and assets within the family, and I also knew that I would stand to inherit very little. I was not from a family of careful savers like he was.

"What about the pets?" I whispered, I knew that that may have sounded strange, but whilst the solicitor had been talking to me about who would get the 10k sports car, and who may get the expensive waterbed, and the processes we would have to go through, all I could think of was making sure that I could keep my horses and my cat, and we somehow came to an agreement over the dogs.

"Don't worry" she laughed "pretty much every modern case I deal with like yours has these same challenges, you can either agree to split the pets and you have some and he has some, or you can agree to a joint custody, like with children."

I felt pacified.

"Is Lazer likely to be very valuable?" she pondered "Not really no, only to me, why?" I felt puzzled.

"Because if she were from very desirable breeding, or training, and likely to be valuable in monetary terms then we would have to list her as an asset, it would be the same with the dogs really."

I laughed "No pretty much all Heinz 57, worth everything to me though."

"Yes, I can tell" she agreed and smiled.

I felt very comfortable with this lady. Although I was in a state of shock and horror about what was unfolding around me, and the reality of getting ready to sell and split everything that Mark and I owned, the solicitor had asked and answered some very serious questions for me.

"What I will do next is write to you, and in turn to Mark, to make your case official" she explained. "Then I would suggest you wait a while, as from what you have said it seems quite clear that your husband does not really know what he wants."

As I left the solicitors offices in agreement with what had been discussed I walked off down the cobbled streets, back to the car park, and I felt just a tiny bit safer.

I had made this official, put costs aside, and started to protect what was mine, from a man who I no longer knew, and no longer trusted, who had given me everything, and yet taken it all away again.

A night with Carol and Patrick

The thought of not being a part of Marks family any more hurt constantly. Knowing he was living at his Mum and Dads made it worse. I kept in touch with Carol by text, almost every few hours, and she was perceptive as to when I needed the support most.

She said simply she felt like she was losing a daughter. But after all the years and memories, I knew we would always stay in touch, too much had been shared between us to have it any other way .But that didn't stop it hurting. I enjoyed being a part of their unit. I was scared by the idea that someone might come in and replace me.

I arranged to go over to their house one evening, it was a Saturday night and I knew that Mark was going out into town with friends, so I could talk to them alone.

I parked up outside their house, at the end of the drive. Normally when I visited this house I had Mark with me, and if I didn't then I knew I would be seeing him soon. And here I was outside the house he was now living in. I started to sweat for a moment, what if he hadn't gone out? What if he was inside somewhere?

But I had nothing to worry about. Carol was waiting for me in the kitchen with open arms. We fell into each others embraces and I cried and cried.

We went through to the large dining / lounge area and Patrick was waiting for me and hugged me.

As they were talking about what had been going on over the last few weeks, I started to realise that they were as mixed up about the whole situation as I was.

Carol told me about the many conversations she had with Mark, trying to get to the bottom of things, and struggling. She knew how he was unhappy, but reminded him that we had everything together. Carol had told Mark that a new person won't be able to give him the memories of all of the years, or the loyalties.

Carol had however agreed with Mark that a new girlfriend or partner or even just a fling would be a very attractive prospect. They may look great, attractive, they may be glamorous, with an amazing figure and there will be new experiences to have, but when all is said and done every relationship will have problems. Nothing and nobody is perfect and eventually you will discover things about everyone that you don't quite like, the grass isn't always greener. It sounded as if she had really been talking sense to him. But in my head I could see Mark, probably sitting where I was sitting and giving Carol; and Patrick lip service, listening to what they said to him, but silently disagreeing.

Patrick was quieter and more thoughtful. He was disappointed that we had apparently given up on our marriage, after only five years.

He hadn't wanted me to go to the solicitors, and when I told him I had already been and met with them for a first consultation, he was not in agreement with my actions, and was concerned that solicitors would just waste all of our money.

"Ruth, I actually don't think Mark would, but if he did, we will protect you, you know that we will make sure that he doesn't take you for a ride financially?" Patrick wanted to make me feel safe, and take care of things.

"I know you will, and I will think about it, but for me, I feel like I don't know him anymore, so this isn't the man that I trust and I just don't know what he is capable of" I said quietly, but firmly.

As I said the words I could tell it was upsetting both of them, and they wanted to deny what I was saying, but they also knew why I felt the way that I did, and that I was trying to protect myself as best as I could.

I sat in their beautiful cream lounge in the lamplight and told them how I had arranged to see some estate agents, and get my own bank account and started to plan what I would do next with a possible divorce. The three of us all sat in the room, not quite able to take it all in, it was such a surreal experience being sat with Marks parents having these discussions because none of us thought there would ever be a need for them.

As I drove away from their house I was emotionally exhausted and ready for sleep, I had a journey home without any music on, and felt a little bit happier.

I shouldn't have married you

It was a very hot Sunday morning.

I was dressed in my cream jodhpurs and a cotton vest, getting saddles and bridles out of my truck, preparing to ride in the field, and planning to bath both horses afterwards.

It is always nice to get them clean and then let them dry off properly in the sun, on a warm day without the risk of them catching a chill.

I had also taken the dogs to the yard, who were playing with their toys, chewing them up and creating a trail of stuffing, in one of the stables.

I had been at the yard about half an hour and was searching for the horse shampoo in the barn, happy to be in the shade for a few moments.

I had heard a familiar noise. It was the noise of Marks car exhaust coming thundering down the lane to the stables. As I came out of the barn I could see a cloud of sand billowing out behind his Mitsubishi Evo as it churned up the ground, Mark was coming at a pace and with purpose.

I had started to sweat. My mouth was drying again and my stomach had started to do little flips. I didn't know if I was excited or afraid, as all the hairs prickled up on the back of my neck. My hackles were up and ready.

Mark came around the corner of the stable yard with the dogs bouncing up at him with joy.

"I thought you would be riding on such a nice day?" he asked. I smiled, "Yes I am going to shortly I think, just doing a few little jobs first."

Mark leant back on the stand which the tap was bolted to and folded his tattooed arms across his chest. I leaned back onto the front of the truck bonnet, folding my own arms, mirroring him for a moment.

"Ruth a load of money is gone from the joint account" He stated aggressively.

"OK, right, how much?" I asked cautiously "I have been writing everything down at home you know, if you tell me how much it is then I can tell you what it is for?"

Mark started going through what he thought was missing "Well, there was a hundred and forty quid in cash yesterday, and about sixty odd quid went out the day before."

Mark was getting irritated for some reason; I could hear it is in his voice. I felt like I needed to explain myself.

"I spent some money at the supermarket, and then I had to pay two months' rent for this place" I gestured to the stables.

"Why Ruth? Why did you have to pay two months in one go?" Marks voice had raised and he was shouting.

"I forgot to pay last month" I stammered, face to the floor, I dare not look at him; I knew he would be annoyed.

"Well that's just great, well done! What if I needed to spend any money this weekend huh? Well, now I can't because it's all gone you have spent it all and you didn't even talk to me about it first!" He looked angrily at me, his face red, arms still folded.

"Sorry" I said quietly.

"Well, I am getting my own bank account Ruth, and I am going to get a new mobile phone too, I need some things of my own, some space of my own" he paused for a moment and then carried on yelling.

"With a new account we can both pay jointly towards bills like the mortgage and then individually have our own fun with whats left." What a cruel statement. Mark would realise of course that based on my earnings , if I paid half towards every one of our outgoings I would have very little change. But in that hellish moment in time it was little of my concern compared to other matters.

"OK ,cool, I am already arranging to get my own account too, that's fine" I was trying to pacify him. I wished he would be pleased that I was taking the initiative over my finances, something I had never done before in our time together and now I prayed that this would impress him.

But I could tell by his body language that this wasn't the end of the conversation; he was not done with me yet. He looked almost menacing.

I gulped and swallowed and started to feel faint. I felt like someone was pouring little shards of ice down my back and all the little hairs all over my body stood on end. I stared at the ground again, I could not bear to look at that angry face.

"Is this why you are so mad Mark, and why you need to leave? Because you need your own bank account? Do you think we will be happier if we split all the finances?" I wished to reason with him.

"Oh no Ruth, it's much deeper than that. It is everything. I need my own money, my own bank account, and I need to spend more time with MY friends, over the years we have always spent all the time with YOUR friends, you never liked me going out with my friends and now I have lost touch with them all and that's because of you, because you made that happen."

He was ranting now, pacing from the yard to the barn, waving his strong arms in the air, occasionally pulling at the hair on the top of his head. His face was red with fury, but his eyes were cold.

"You always stopped us having children Ruth, you always kept moving the goal posts. You are to blame. First you wanted to be married and then you wanted a bigger house, and a better job, the list is endless it just went on and on and one, with me giving you everything you ever needed and asked for, and you wouldn't give me the one thing I really needed."

Thoughts that had been haunting Mark were tumbling out, the words rushed from his mouth , bounced across the ground and stung and bit me as they reached my ears. I would not be able to silence this tirade.

I looked at his distraught face. I felt terrible. I had done this. Raw guilt poured all over me in cold form. He was of course right. I was the gatekeeper and we were still childless as I still struggled not feeling safe or ready to start a family.

"You tricked me Ruth. You made me think that one day it would happen, but you just kept putting me off. I gave you everything you asked for, answered every request. But it still didn't happen, it was just a trick."

Mark had started marching out of the barn towards his car. He opened the large metal green gates that keep the yard safe, swinging them with all his strength until they bounced back smashing into shrubs, clattering loudly as they went. Mia and Phoenix were hiding under some hay bales in the barn, Mia was shaking, neither of them dared to move.

"But what about our vows Mark? Maybe I just wasn't ready yet? Can't we just talk about this some more?" I could hear the pathetic wining in my voice, but I hadn't got a stronger version of myself anymore, he had demolished me.

Mark started to open the driver's door to his car; he turned and look back at me, and started to speak, his voice filled with twelve years of regret and venom.

"I should never have got married Ruth. I shouldn't have married you. It wasn't what I wanted. I never wanted any of this. This is what you wanted."

Before I could say another word he leapt into his car, shut the door with all his force, making a heavy bang and started the engine. He went speeding off down the lane, again a sandy cloud behind the evolution, the loud exhaust echoing the loud and angry words Mark had left behind him.

I walked back onto the yard, gently closing the large gates.

I flopped into the barn and the dogs ran over to me, as I crumpled to the floor, falling into the strewn about hay. The world spun around me as I used every last scrap of energy to cry and cry and cry, until it felt as if my heart was actually breaking, ripping open my chest, the physical pain was immense as I wept into the dogs fur.

I don't know how long I lay in the hay on the stone floor in the barn. I don't know if I was conscious the whole time or part of it.

The sun started to creep in and warm me, and I looked up out of the barn, past my truck to the field where the horses were staring back at me over the wooden rails. Maybe they were concerned or just curious as to what all the fuss had been about.

I fumbled in my jodhpurs pocket for my phone and dialled.

"Mum, Mark has been here and he said that he never wanted to marry me, that he blames me that we didn't have children……I don't know what to do."

My voice trailed away.

"Ruth, where are you?" she asked calmly.

"I'm at the yard" I managed weakly.

"Listen to me Ruth, I am putting my shoes on now, and I will be there as soon as I can. It's going to be ok."

I fell to the floor again, as if my legs were made of jelly.

I called Carol and told her what had happened. Most of what I was saying was a babbling mess.

"I am sorry; I just couldn't stay strong anymore, not with him saying those things."

"Ruth it's OK, shush, I don't know what is wrong with him. I am going to have a talk with him when he gets back, and tell him to leave you alone, I am really sorry that this has had to happen , even I feel like I don't know my own son anymore."

I could hear Patrick in the background. He must have been listening to the conversation. He was raging in the distance.

"Are you on your own ? Shall we come over now?" Carol asked, I could hear the concern in her voice.

"No, it's OK, thanks, mum is coming."

I said goodbye to them and went back to sitting on the floor.

I heard Marks words over and over in my head; he should never have married me. As if as he says the words, he takes it all away, there was no wedding day, it doesn't exist, or at least he didn't want it to. He pours out his truths and erases all of our happy memories.

By the time mum arrived I was a sandy, dirty mess. The top of my vest was soaked with sweat and tears and I couldn't get up off the floor. My Mum is only a small woman, but she found some hidden super strength to pull me right up to my feet.

"He never wanted to marry me mum, and I stopped him having children, he gave me everything and I didn't give him the one things he wanted" I couldn't breathe anymore, I had cried and shouted every last bit of air from my lungs, the world started to go by as I was in my mother's arms, maybe at last I was actually dying and he had finally killed me.

But no, a force was dragging me and shaking my whole body and slapping my face.

"No. I won't let him do this to you, do you hear me. You are not beholden to him anymore, and you shan't be. I don't want you to listen to a word more of that rubbish. I was there when Mark married you, and every piece of him wanted to be there, in that winery on that cliff top. He chose it all much as you. That may no longer be how he feels, but on that day he wanted that more than anything. "

The slap still burned on my cheek and the shaking had woken me. I was breathing again. I was stood on the stable yard in the warm sunshine. Mark had nearly killed me but Mum wouldn't let me go.

"Now I don't think riding when you are like this is a very good idea at all Ruth, that mare will walk all over you in this fragile state, so pop your trainers on and we will take the dogs for a nice walk."

I didn't have anything else to say. I just watched mum reach into the back of my truck, get the dogs leads and pop them around their necks as she handed me my trainers and car keys.

We walked for miles across fields which had had their grass cut and turned; ready to be baled up, probably the same bales that I would buy as the summer turned to autumn. The dogs had a lovely time running in and out of large piles of cut grass, and Mum talked to me softly with stories about what my brothers had been doing to annoy her, and what her cats had been up to.

It was everything that I needed right then at that moment in time and it saved me. By the time we get back to the stable yard it was evening.

One of the other women who kept her horse at the yard had arrived to do a feed.

"Gosh Ruth, you have lost some weight, you look amazing" she exclaimed genuinely.

"Thanks" I replied, surprised by what she had said. Looking down I realised that my once tight jodhpurs were hanging off me.

Mum steered me away from the other women as we went into the barn and mixed up the evening feeds for my horses.

"Come on darling" she said breezily as she moved me and the dogs off the stable yard and into the field, to feed Lazer and Charlie, away from the other prying conversations.

Once the horses had been fed and checked mum supervised me into the truck with the dogs, and followed me back to my house in her car.

Parking up we went inside for one of her many daily cups of tea.

"I want you to promise me something darling, I really want you to try to stop allowing Mark to come and see you like this. It's destroying you."

"I know mum, but I need to see him."

"Not like this you don't Ruth."

I knew she was right. I knew that when he turned up at the house or the stable yard I should just ask him to leave, but I couldn't seem to do it.

"I'm going now, please eat something and try to get some sleep. And call me anytime that you need to. We all love you very much."

She hugged me and kissed me as she got into her car, and I stood on the drive and waved her off, down the street.

She hadn't been gone long when Carol called.

"We have spoken to Mark. He said that he had been coming to the stable yard to see the horses because he, missed them, he didn't think that you would be there."

"Oh" I said, feeling muddled. Followed by "But I am always there."

"We know, Patrick has been very angry with Mark, he said that it was guaranteed you would be there, he went out of his way to come and see you. Of all the places you could be, going to the stables was always a sure bet."

I was comforted in some way that even they were puzzled by Marks behaviour.

After we had said goodbye I went upstairs and peeled off my sweaty and stinky clothes, letting them pile up on the floor of the ensuite. I stepped into the shower and let the water run. I felt like the hot trickles were cleansing me of all the days traumas. As I started to wash I could almost feel my ribs. Looks like my friend at the stables was right, I thought, I am losing weight.

I smiled to myself as I washed. At least I was in control of something.

The day after

Somewhere within me I had to muster the energy and strength to go to work. To pretend like the day before had never happened.

I was exhausted but I managed to get out of bed, make strong, black coffee, sort out all the pets and drove over to the office.

On the journey to the office I started thinking that if I could be a fake version of myself I could perhaps escape the reality going on inside my head and my heart.

I sat at my desk going through emails and looking at some planning documents for new projects. I refused to let my mind wander. Shutting out the voices in my head. No Mark. No comments about how I can never be what he wants, and how he never should have married me. Just me and my work, delivering service to clients, that's all that would have to matter.

The sales director, Peter, wanted a sales meeting. This was normal practise for Monday mornings.

Elaine would make coffee, open a packet of biscuits (as a sweetener) and Peter would get James, Mary and I to go through the last weeks sales figures, see if we had any clients with immediate issues and what the plan of attack would be for the forthcoming week.

He would then report to the other directors, who would be generally dissatisfied with whatever we had said, and usually a whole range of other meetings would ensue. It was a ridiculous puppet show, with the owners having us all jiggling about on our little strings.

Peter sat us all down in a business-like fashion.

"Right then team let's have a catch up!" He was enthusiastic to try and make up for the facade. Nobody said anything back in response to him, so he carried on. "Well I had a lovely weekend, I played some golf, my wife made me a lovely Sunday dinner and I went to watch my son play some football, and as you will see I caught the sun a little."

We all laughed at his pink face.

Peter turned expectantly to James.

"Well, I went out on Friday and Saturday night, and spent Sunday on the garden recovering."

We all laughed again, and now we turned to Mary.

"I took my daughter to the cinema with her friends, and then they had a sleepover, which basically means I didn't get any sleep, so I'm a bit knackered" she smiled.

They all turned to me. I started to prickle around my face and blush. My palms were sweating and I couldn't swallow. I should make something up, there was no way I could tell them all the truth, not this way, not these people, I didn't want my colleagues to know my personal and private affairs, I was searching , struggling, my mind was blank and I could think of nothing. The silent gap I could not fill.

"Ruth, what did you get up to?" Peter grinned at me.

"Mark came to the field and shouted at me and told me he was getting his own bank account, and that I had tricked him and he didn't want the house he didn't want to be married and it's all my fault we didn't have children" I shouted, and collapsed onto the circular meeting room table in a torrent of tears. Everyone stared at me. Embarrassed and disgraced, the last place where my troubles couldn't follow me was broken. The cold feeling was at work with me in the meeting room.

I felt as if I was a million miles away watching the horrific scene play out, where people who I didn't really trust got to be a part of my intimate feelings.

"Oh Ruth, I'm so sorry, I thought you were coping all of this time, you seemed to be doing do well" Peter put an arm around me and passed me a tissue. He waved James and Mary away out of the meeting room behind us.

"Come on now, don't let John and Jane see you like this, you are stronger than that."

Peter managed to cheer me up with a silly tale of how he got drunk whilst watching his son play football, and his wife told him off. The story made a good filler whilst my tears dried and then it was safe to release me back into the main sales office with my colleagues

He called the other two directors into the meeting room, so he could do his usual weekly report.

Once they were all locked away in the meeting room, Mary held me to her bosom and let me cry on her until her blouse was wet with my tears and smeared with thick, black mascara.

"They are all bastards Ruth" she said firmly "I just don't know what is wrong with Mark, but if I see him I will tan his arse" she stated in her warm Irish accent.

I smiled back at my friend. She too had split up with her partner recently, the father of her child. We were both now part of a club we never wanted to belong to, the newly singles club.

The conversations that other people were always having, that I never thought would happen to me, yet there I was.

And now I had opened the flood gates in the office and exposed my real vulnerability. I couldn't hide anywhere from my feelings anymore.

More Counselling sessions

After Mark had been to the horse's yard on the Sunday and killed me again I was in more desperate need than ever to see the councillor.

I had gotten to the point where I couldn't really concentrate. My mouth felt constantly dry, I was grinding my teeth, chewing my lip, and again, eating very little.

I knew the drill. I had been to see the councillor a few times now. I knew that we would go up the staircases to the counselling room, and I would tell her all that had happened.

The events of the last week tumbled from me. Her pretty face crinkling, into patterns of increasing concern.

"How do you feel that Mark keeps coming back like this?" she chose her words carefully.

"He tells you that he is leaving you, that he wants to be alone, but then he comes back all the time?"

She questioned softly.

"I think it's because he needs to see the dogs" I whispered, I didn't know if that was the only reason, but I knew it was a factor.

"Well Ruth, I think you need to tell him that he should arrange with you when he is going to come back for his possessions, or to see the dogs, because we need to limit the damage he is causing you by keep coming back like this. You need to keep your relationship with him almost as if he were a colleague or someone you were doing business with so you can make formal meeting times, and you can prepare yourself better that way, or choose not to be there."

I knew in my head she was right, oh yes, she spoke logic, and this would be the absolute best way forward, but in my heart I doubted I could ever control Mark well enough to have that power. I probably didn't want to? My will power wasn't strong enough either. He was calling the shots and I was letting him. I never voiced those thoughts to her. Silently they ticked through my mind.

"How do you feel about all that he said to you on Sunday?" She ventured.

"I feel angry and confused and upset " I responded.

"Good Ruth, because I am angry and confused on your part. I think you do need to try and suggest to him that he seeks help if you at all can" She explained "But my main concern is your heath and what it is doing to you every time he keeps coming back like this."

If he didn't keep coming back, I wouldn't see him…….

We changed our focus, and started to look at some of the notes I had made, some of the research I had done into why I felt angry.

The councillor was interested in all that I had written. Aspects of life that I had written down that I was supposedly angry about, from disputes with my parents as a teenager, to feeling like I had failed training my young horse. Everything I thought could be a cause for my sometimes volatile and furious outbursts was written down in black and white.

I had been looking for something as I wrote. An answer. But I wasn't looking to discover why I was angry. I was looking to find an answer to why Mark had left me.

Despite my inner feelings the councillor was very encouraging and said that I was insightful into my behaviours, and that dealing with things I have perhaps never dealt with properly was helping me.

In reality many months down the line, I did realise that although these activities were helpful, and I did finally loose some demons, they weren't the real issue; they were merely a distraction.

The key focus remained the turmoil I was going through, still in complete disbelief that I had failed and my marriage was over, and the deep sadness and frustration that Mark had left and I would never really know why.

Months on, I realised that the councillor was giving me coping strategies. She had been teaching me how to deal with bad situations.

She couldn't change what had happened, and she couldn't change what was going to happen. But she could change how I dealt with things.

The day Mum and I went to the seaside

Once again a week had gone by at work, and I felt relived as the weekend came. Mum and I decided to take the dogs to play at the seaside for the day.

There had been a strong wind blowing and it felt like it was freshening my head, silencing the voices. Mia and Phoenix had a lovely time chasing the waves and each other.

Mum and I also met up with Kathryn and her parents at the seaside with George; they were doing the same thing.

All of us had gone to escape the life's we had become trapped in, desperate for some respite.

The warm sea breeze and the miles of beach, and walking until we were all exhausted it gave our souls the cleansing they were looking for.

When we were home later, mum had hugged me and kissed me and then left to drive home, whilst I focused on cleaning the sand out of my car. I was busy shaking towels and wiping salt water off the windows of the truck when I heard a voice, it was one of the neighbours from across the street.

I hadn't spoken to her much in the time we had lived on the estate, but we knew each others names and would often say hello in passing.

"He has left you hasn't he?" Her tone was sympathetic but loud, I dreaded that everyone would hear. I'm not a fan of dirty laundry in public, 'please nobody hear' I said inside my head.

"Yes, he has he said that doesn't want to be with me anymore, we were together 12 years and all of a sudden we are not anymore" my voice tapered away. It wasn't a discussion I wanted to have.

"Well, I thought I would come and tell you that the same thing happened to me when I was about your age, and I felt terrible, but after a while of being away from me he came back."

I was intrigued. It turned out that she had experienced something very similar, but it hadn't all ended in disaster in fact, quite the contrary, it had made them stronger.

I went back in the house and felt something I had not felt in a long time. I don't know if it was the long journey driving, the sea air or the neighbour's kind words, but I felt relaxed.

I lay on the sofa with the dogs. I pondered my new friends words and coupled them with what Michael at the feed shop had said, there was a small yet shiny sliver of hope left. I just needed to make Mark feel safe.

I sent Mark a text message

"Thank you for all that you have done for me, thank you for giving me this fairy-tale life, with all the things I could have ever wanted and more."

I didn't get a reply to my message, but I did drop off to sleep. A very deep sleep, and stayed asleep on the sofa until morning, snuggled up with my two loyal friends.

In the garage

He was there again.

I sat on the bottom step in the house listening to the noise from the adjoining garage, wishing that this wasn't happening.

The more things Mark took away to his new life, away from me, to be with his parents, the more real the separation became. I had been back to the solicitors and spoken to estate agents. All the physical objects and possessions would begin to be pulled away from our castle, yet the person, and his emotions kept returning.

I went into the kitchen and stared out of the large windows. I looked out to the view of fields that spread for miles one way, and then more large detached houses like ours the other way.

The glittering caught my eye. The kitchen had three very large windows and we had to have a bespoke blind to fit all the way across. The blind was sparkling, metallic blue, to match the worktops.

I looked down at the worktops, and the breakfast bar. The fitted cupboards. The expensive knife block and mug tree.

Another room of things that Mark and I had designed and decided on together, which would be lost and no longer ours when the house was sold. It wouldn't be full of us and our belongings anymore.

I swallowed hard as Mark came into the kitchen.

He looked at me, I don't know if he saw the tears in my eyes, but he looked at me sympathetically.

For once Mark didn't look angry.

"I am really sorry that its come to this Ruth you know" he said maybe reading my thoughts "but I did realise when I was outside the house that day, I wanted to walk the dogs with someone, to have someone to do things with of an evening, and you were always with the horses, I could never see you without them, they have become so expensive and time consuming you just throw everything at them, and I felt like I was always last on your list of priorities."

I looked down at the tiled floor, the tears clouding my vision, as he had my achilles again, using something I really loved as a reason why he was leaving, making me feel like I had to choose, but maybe I already had. I gulped back more tears as the cold feeling poured itself down my neck and all the breath went out of me.

"You weren't the only one who felt that Mark, I wanted to spend time with you, to do things together, go out in the evenings, out for the day on Sundays, walk the dogs with you, but you never suggested them either. You weren't the only one who felt like this."

He looked back at me as I stared at him. Stood in the hallway we had reached a similar conclusion. For that moment we had realised we were both guilty of not putting time aside for the other person. And both of us had felt the same and neither of us had said anything.

I decided to say something that was deep within me whilst I had the chance.

"When Barney died I thought that nothing could ever be any worse, nothing could be worse than losing one of your best friends, going through hell every day preying that he could come back, but I realise now that I was wrong, there was something much worse. This is worse than death, it goes on and on and on and I feel like I cannot cope with it anymore" I was screaming by that point. "So maybe that will go some way towards making you know that not everything is about the horses to me."

Mark said nothing. He looked at my face and then at the floor, and then at the door. He needed an exit.

"Well, I am sorry" that was all he said, and then he closed the door quietly, and I heard him drive away. Driven from me again by a truthful outburst too ugly and harsh to accept.

I walked into the lounge. On the mantelpiece there were several photographs. One was of my beloved pony Barney, who died, and another right next to it was Mark and I smooching at our wedding reception. He was bending me back into a strong and dominant embrace, his lips on mine.

I had thought about similarities in the way the pictures made me feel. Barney died, but Mark may as well have also died, because the man I knew and loved had gone. It was as if he died within and left, and someone else took over his body.

The night of the police helicopter

I had been trying to sleep , snuggled up in bed with the dogs for comfort. I had the purple duvet pulled over my head to block out the late evening sun. The pink curtains were thin, and let the light through them even though they were firmly drawn. I had the windows wide open to try and let some breeze into the warm house. I had turned in early, about 9, exhausted after another day at work pretending to cope and an evening of Marks voice in my head and wresting with emotions.

I recall being able to hear a sound in the distance, like the beat of low blades propelling round, a helicopter? Then some shouting.

Phoenix barked. We all sat up in bed, fully awake and startled.

The noise got louder and louder. I could hear sirens too.

Curiosity overcame tiredness and I got up and looked out of the window. Two men were running furiously across the field that backed on to the garden.

The helicopter must have been directly over the house at that point. The spinning blades were deafeningly loud.

I ran downstairs, worrying where Pharoah cat was. I had left the windows open because of the heat, and she would often sneak out onto the roof, and drop down to the fence and then carefully onto the garden. I imagined that all the noise would startle her. I flung the patio doors open and ran straight outside onto the rear lawn. I looked up in the dusky light and I could see the pilots in the helicopter it was so low. I could even see one of them talking into his mouthpiece.

I could also see uniformed officers in the field next to the house, running along, and assumed they must be chasing the men I saw before them.

I suddenly had a moment of realisation that I was outside in my pyjamas and dressing gown. I looked to the house next door. An elderly couple were also outside in their pyjamas. It was the same at the house next door to them. I realised with amusement that because this was a quiet area with low crime, none of us was accustomed to this sort of disturbance, so we had all gone outside to see what the commotion was about, in our tartan checks and floral nighties.

I also started to think that we may have a false sense of security as well, if the men I had seen were still on the loose there was a high chance that they may run onto the garden. I didn't know if they were dangerous, or armed with weapons, or even why they were being chased, although did wonder with such a high police presence it probably wasn't something good!

Pharoah cat had darted out of some long grass probably waiting to pounce on a victim, and I saw my opportunity and grabbed her up into my arms and called the dogs. We fled back inside. I locked the utility door. I checked the patio doors and the front door. I checked every single latch and window lock.

I was shaking. Beyond the amusement of being outside in my pyjamas was the realisation that I was alone and felt vulnerable. There was no man at the house to protect me.

I wanted to tell Mark what has happened. I told him everything.

Or at least I did once.

He would always make me feel safe. Protecting me, wrapping his strong arms around me, cocooning me in his embrace,he fought away physical and emotional threats, he was my rock.

Maybe I could just drop him a text message? I picked up my phone. That was not the actions of the strong woman everyone had told me to be. This was the weak and feeble woman. I could hear all of the voices in my head, a hundred reasons I shouldn't press send. But I did it anyway.

"Police helicopter over house, men being chased in field next to garden…quite scary!"

I got an almost instant reply .."Just stay inside Ruth…make sure you stay inside."

That was all I got. It wasn't what I hoped for. There was no offer of coming to be my protector and keep me from harm. No King to protect his Queen and his castle, and no seeming interest or concern in the situation. I felt crushed, knowing that all the care in Mark for me, and what we owned and our pets was gone. He was not coming.

Was I really afraid of the men in the field? Or was I far more terrified of the hold I no longer had over my own man? Mark came and went when he pleased. He would no longer be persuaded by me, not for protection or otherwise. He no longer was my man.

I slid under the duvet and closed my eyes, listening to the propellers of the helicopter spin, mixed with sirens and shouting. Even with the windows firmly shut and locked, I could still hear all the noises, and of course I was listening harder for them now.

Time passed and the din of the blades and police cars started to fade and move away.

I shut my eyes tighter still and took slow breaths. I remembered once being told not to count sheep, just to remember the one sheep, keep thinking of one consistent sheep. The imaginary creature in my mind trotted back and forth, looking for ways to escape its paddock……opening its mouth with baa……baaa

The sheep was interrupted by a sound from reality ,a modified car exhaust and dump valves. It burbled along, and appeared to come to a halt at the end of the close, pausing only for a few seconds, I could hear the car drive down to roundabout at the end of the street and stop. Before quickly starting up again and driving away.

Was it Mark? Did he come to check after all? Did he still want to defend his Queen and his Castle?

I sent him a message again.

"Were you just outside the house?"

"No it wasn't me."

But I was so sure, it sounded just like his car, the tone of his nurspec exhaust and the sound of his dump valves. So why come here and not actually come to the house?

It was a scenario I would only ever have my suspicions about and not actually know the truth.

The day of the football

I have never been a big football lover. I don't feel inspired by the game and I probably pass unfair judgement over the perceived lifestyle. When my siblings and I were growing up we were encouraged to play sports, but none of us really took to the soccer scene.

Casting this aside, if a major game was playing then it was seen as an excellent excuse for a family gathering. Just as the match would bring a team and its supporters together as one it was inspiration for family unity. Food and drink and relaxing .This particular day we needed no further encouragement, and having had such a hideous few weeks, not just for me, but for my closest family members, it felt good to be organising a fun activity together. I wanted to host, I craved the company and my loyal family were only too happy to oblige.

I had been to visit the horses at the yard in the early afternoon, and went to the local shop on the way back through the village, to collect some beers and snacks, I knew what my brothers wanted in advance and had my list prepared.

I was asked for ID in the shop, which was curious, been as I was nearly 30. I recall looking at myself in the shop mirror, my ghostly face with straggled hairs stuck to my dirty and sweaty forehead, and my loose jeans, falling from my waist where they no longer sat. I didn't look young so much as out of place, like I no longer belonged to my own existence.

Back at the house I took a shower, hoping to wash my worries away. I stacked the beers in the fridge. I clicked the top off my first and took a long swig and closed my eyes for a moment, the bottle almost sticking to my hand it was so cold.

I was lying back on the garden at our first house, we had no chairs, we were laying on old bath towels, they were like cardboard with years of use, the material pricking my skin, but I didn't care as I swilled the cool beer and closed my eyes as Marks lips were on mine, alone at last in our new safe haven. He gently had both of my hands under one of his arms, pushing me harder into the lawn reminding me I was his as I willingly accepted his commands.

I awake form my daydream as the front door crashed open.

Mum has arrived with the brothers in tow. They all wrapped their arms around me, and I felt safe in the middle of a Jack and Kit bubble. It's funny how I had two younger brothers, and could remember carrying them about in my arms, but all these years later when I felt so small and weak and vulnerable , I became aware that they both towered over me it was me who needed to be picked up.

We had drawn the curtains, tuned up the TV and created a den for ourselves in the lounge with our beers (except for Mum who was carefully guarding her cup of tea.) We all exchanged glances as we heard another car pull up on the drive. Peeping back behind the curtains I could see that it was Marks works van.

The cold feeling trickled from the top of my head down into my toes. My mouth went dry. I didn't know how this would unfold, and how this group of people would now react to each other. I feared hostility between the parties.

I sat back into the sofa, glancing at Mum, who looked at me in a concerned stare. The dogs went bouncing out of the room to greet Mark as he wandered down the hallway into the kitchen. I heard the tap go on as he got himself a drink.

"Hi" he poked his head around the corner into the lounge. "you all OK?"

"Yes thanks Mark, how are you?" Mum answered politely.

My brothers said nothing, Jack turned around in his chair and looked at Mark, his face deep in thought, but he said nothing. Kit didn't even turnaround from the TV screen. Both boys abandoned by their older brother in law who had left me and them in turn. The room was thick with their anger over the devastation and pain he was causing me.

I have never felt so much pride and anguish at the same time. Proud of my brothers, realising that they were growing up, and were capable of making up their own minds. And they had both judged that they didn't wish to speak to Mark. I was proud that I felt their protection. But for Mark I felt the anguish. That the little brothers he had known since they were 4 and 7 were suddenly punishing him with their silence.

Mark looked coldly into the room and then walked back out into the kitchen and down the hallway.

I followed him to the garage, like a lost soul. Unable to ignore him and I didn't have the strength to punish him like the others, I just wanted him back.

"So how are you then?" I asked cautiously "Yea, I'm good, I've just come to get some bits for a job tomorrow" his body language seemed relaxed, methodically, piling pieces of cable and trunking into the back of his white van, arranging tools into the racking as he went.

"You can stay and watch the football with all of us you know" I ventured softly, feeling guilty that I had taken over the house with my family, and worried that Mark may feel excluded and have nowhere to go.

"No, it's fine, I don't think I am very welcome in there Ruth, it's quite clear that your family all hate me."

"That's not true Mark, they are worried about you" I replied, my voice sounding feeble.

As we stood outside talking I could hear cheering on the telly speakers, over the progress with the football presumably and more cheering coming out of my lounge. I peeked in from outside, my brothers were sprawled across the comfy sofas and chairs, with the dogs on their knees, splashing beer around happily. What I would give to be able to add Mark back to this scene. How it always was, all of us like one big family. But lines had been crossed.

A smiling face appeared at the front door, to beckon me back in.

"Come on Ruth, you are missing all the fun, I've opened you another beer" said my normally teetotal and none alcohol approving mother, as she put her arms around me and pushed me gently back into the house. "Bye Mark" she said softly, as she shut the door behind us, passed me the icy cold drink and popped me back into the lounge. Almost like a mother hen returning one of her chicks to the safety of the nest.

My brothers and my mum all looked at each other and smiled as I sat down with them. Happy that they had captured me from further torturing myself.

As Mark drove away another goal was scored and we were all cheering and laughing.

The match finished and mum made some fresh pizzas which we all munched on, and I was grateful that the beers had given me some sort of an appetite. It was not the weight loss I worried about , I was pleased with the slimmer me, it was the constant exhaustion from the lack of fuel in my tired system.

Mum, Kit and I were sat around the dining table chatting, and Jack was outside on a deck chair humming to himself, with a beer in one hand, and a roll-up in the other. Kit and I smiled at each other as we smelt the suspiciously sweet smell of the contents of Jacks cigarette wafting in through the open patio doors. Mum either didn't notice or couldn't face any conflict. Almost as if everyone was so depleted at the goings on of the last few weeks, some things were being let go of.

As dusk started to fall we set off for a walk into the woods. We walked up the steep stony track in the forests. The dogs rushed through the thick undergrowth mostly unseen by us, every now and again we would catch a brief glimpse of them between leaves and grasses.

We arrived at one of my favourite places, a massive clearing up in the woods, the view stretched for miles around. Villages, farms, field after field, wood after wood. The different areas making a patchwork of greens, browns and yellows in the summer months, and it was truly beautiful. The last piece of the days sun warmed us as we stood up on top of the hill and took in the panoramic experience.

Jack climbed a small mound to get a better view, but unfortunately the alcohol consumption had clouded his judgement and he disappeared off the other side as we all laughed.

Having picked Jack up and dusted him down we walked further into the thicket.

"I think it's this way" I poked the air with my finger, not really sure.

"Oh dear, you don't know do you?" questioned Kit

"Oh well, let's go this way anyway" Jack stomped into the undergrowth the way I had pointed, and we all went a little further, following his lead, we could see some light the way we were headed, the dogs cutting the way for us as they bounced past enthusiastically.

"Ouch" mum said from behind me.

"Ouch from me too" I squealed.

We had all wondered into the biggest pile of stinging nettles and little sore bumps came up quickly on our bare arms and legs.

We ran out of the coppice into another clearing, laughing hysterically at each other's almost wart like skin caused by the nettles.

We somehow managed to stumble home, and Mum discovered some cream in her handbag to help with the rashes. We all applied it gratefully and somewhat liberally.

"I'm going home now darling" she declared gently as she hugged me "but I am leaving these two here to look after you."

"OK, thanks Mum" I smiled back

After Mum had been waved off we all made ourselves comfortable on the sofa with some more beers.

"I just don't understand Mark" said Kit profoundly "I just don't understand why he is doing this to you, why leave everything now, so suddenly" Kit was young, I had assumed commitment was something he wouldn't even consider, yet at 16 years old the puzzle didn't even make sense to him.

"I don't know, I just don't know, I thought we were so happy" Was all I could manage.

"Well I don't think it's fair that he keeps coming back like this" said Jack. "It's not fair on you, it's like he has you on a string all of the time and he can just pull it whenever he wants."

I looked at the floor, staring into the beige carpet. I knew what they were saying was true, I shouldn't let Mark control me, I should be stronger, but it was a harsh reality I didn't want to accept. I gulped back the tears; refusing to let the waterworks spoil such a good evening.

"Let's open the Sambuca" was my best suggestion.

I didn't have to say it twice, Jack had already run into the kitchen and helped himself to some shot glasses, whilst Kit reached inside the drinks cabinet.

It was starting to get light again when we eventually decided to go to sleep. But I dropped to sleep easily with my brothers in the house, feeling a little safer, and not so alone.

The day after the football

I could feel the hangover in my head before I even opened my eyes.

The sickly sweet flavour of Sambuca was still on my lips and I felt the alcohol vapours as I breathed in and out.

I could hear Jack and Kit start to stir, both making noises that indicated they felt the same as I did. Regrettable about the level of drink consumption and the hour we had gone to bed.

I got dressed and went downstairs to consider making some breakfast. Having my brothers in the house helped me, it gave me a purpose to get up, and make coffee ,get some cereals out, and put some bread in the toaster, because I knew that they would need to eat. It was good for me to have other people around me.

My Dad had agreed that he would come and collect my brothers from the horse's yard later on in the morning, and glancing at the clock in the kitchen I knew that it was time to force them out of their slumber.

Jack was on the sofa rolled up in a green sleeping bag, looking like a caterpillar. "Hello, I made you some coffee" I said to my very small eyed brother. "Thanks Ruth, that's great" he started to take a sip and sit up on the sofa. I wondered upstairs where Kit was hiding in bed in one of the spare rooms. I lifted the covers slightly to find he was not alone, Mia had got in with him, and Pharaoh cat was napping on a ruffled section at the end at the end of the duvet.

"Coffee?" I asked "Yes" he mumbled, and I noticed I had another small eyed brother.

We all ate some breakfast, played with the dogs, got showered and started to function. Jack became the centre of attention and amusement, when he couldn't understand why he had got out of the shower and was more dirty than he was when he went in and was also covered in thick, coarse hair. It transpired he had used one of the dogs towels to dry himself. He looked confused as he got back into the shower. It was great having the boys in the house, the constant interaction and banter meant the voices in my head didn't have any opportunity to speak. I only had to deal with the present moments.

I drove us all over to the horse's yard. For once it was a cold and overcast day, and it rained intermittently. As our hangovers started to wear off we all feel a bit jaded by reality.

Having fed the horses, the boys and the dogs and I were all sat on some bales of hay in one of the stables. A familiar face popped around the corner of the wooden stable block.

"Morning all " said Dad, formal as ever. "Hello" We all chorused.

It was the first time I had seen Dad since Mark left and I was not sure what he would say.

"Did you all have a good time last night?" Dad asked and then added "I can see you were all fairly well oiled."

"We had an ace time, but Mark tried to ruin it by coming back and messing with Ruth's head again" bitterness sounded in Kit's tone.

"Oh, I see" Dad pondered. Now Jack spoke. "It's just not right, nothing that he says makes sense. He wants to leave and to be happy, but he was happy before, and anyway he just keeps on coming back and not really actually leaving at all!"

As I listened to Jacks words he echoed some of the thoughts that just went around and around in my confused mind.

"Well" started Dad as the voice of reason "I have to say that I think Mark has possibly been unhappy for some time, but he is not really dealing with things at the moment. I recognise his behaviour from dark places I have been myself, he is sort of hiding under the sheets at the moment you see. He knows he is not happy, but when he pokes his head out of the top of the duvet he is not happy with what is there, so he crawls back in."

The boys and I looked at each other wondering about Dad's analogy. "Anyway, I know that you are all hurt and angry and upset, but we have to remember that there is actually a much worse side to all of this, because someone is leaving the family, someone who has been with us for a long time and that is a very sad thing."

With those words I collapsed to the stone floor as Dad grabbed me, stopping me from falling onto the cold wet concrete.

"I just can't do this Dad. I just can't cope with it, it's more than I can manage." All the tears I had hidden from my brothers surfaced. I had suppressed my emotions to protect them, I didn't want them to see their oldest sister all broken and ruined and had stayed strong, but with my father next to me I could let go, I knew he was strong enough to handle seeing me like this, and I couldn't keep the cold feeling inside of me for any longer as I wailed out loud the pain from deep in my heart.

"Bear down on it Ruth" he advised "let yourself feel how you need to feel, if you need to cry, then cry, if you need to scream and shout then just do it, we are all here for you."

I felt as if I was somewhere in the sky, looking down on this scene from above the stable roof. Watching my shrivelled form, with my Dad trying to collect me.

Looking at my younger brothers horrified faces, tears in their down eyes. Powerless. The dogs sat staring at us. I don't know how long we all stayed like that, but I let go until there was no air left in my lungs.

Dad gave me a hug and a kiss before he left with my brothers. "This will all be OK Ruth" I nodded at him, but I didn't believe it. I couldn't see how it would ever be ok.

Kit and Jack hugged me and squashed me, offering to come and stay whenever I needed them.

They drove off down the lane, away from the stable yard.

I went back into the stable where we had all been sat, and curled up on some of the bales of hay with the dogs. I was exhausted; I had nothing left in me. I fell asleep for a while to give my mind some peace from the noise of the voices that were back once I was alone again.

Heart to heart on the stairs

It was a Saturday afternoon. I had been cleaning the house, just a bit of hoovering, I couldn't really be that bothered. I was at a loose end. I had got to the stage where none of the things I loved made me happy anymore, or if they did it was very temporary. The second I left the horse's yard, or got back from a walk with the dogs, or my family left me on my own, the voices began to taunt me, with all the things Mark had said going round and round for me to over analyse.

Food had become just a source of energy to keep going. I didn't fancy alcohol other than to make me sleep. Going out with my friends was not motivational. Riding the horses helped as did walking the dogs, but as soon as I had stopped the physical activity I was back to the place where I thought about things too much again.

It was happening on that Saturday. I knew the house needed cleaning and I thought it would be a welcome distraction but before I realised it I was sat on the stairs daydreaming. The muttering began. Mum talking, Carol talking and Mark talking. People from work talking. They would all speak at the same time getting louder until it was just a spinning in audible mess.

My day dream was broken by the sound of the sports exhaust on the Evo, coming bumbling down the street.

All the usual feelings passed over me. I felt the cold tingle, my mouth was drying and I started to shake. But I didn't move from the steps where I was sitting.

Mark flung the door open, the dogs pouncing on him as usual. We looked at each other and laughed. It was hard not to with the level of enthusiasm he was greeted with.

"Have you come for some work stuff again?" I ask quietly, surprisingly calm for me.

"No actually Ruth, I just came to see you" He said. A tickle of heat passed over me.

He walked over to the bottom of the stairs and sat on the step beneath the one I was perched on.

He was dressed in shorts and a vest, he looked tanned and healthy and was actually smiling for once. His brown eyes looked warm.

"I've had a letter from the solicitors" I updated him "and I've had another letter from all the estate agents following up their visits. You can have a look at them if you like, although I think I have chosen who I would prefer to go with, if that's ok?" I spoke honestly, hating the reality, however was no point in stalling on the inevitable.

"I just don't know how this all happened Ruth. I don't know how we got here."

"I know Mark, I don't either"

I looked into his eyes. He looked hopeless and lost. I felt the same.

Mark started to cry. He changed instantly from happy and relaxed, to tense and emotional.

He suddenly looked so sad. But for once in a long time he didn't not look angry, or like he wanted to blame me. He just looks depressed, struggling to find what would make him happy.

I couldn't bear to see him like that. How could there be no answer for us in all of this mess I wondered?

"It's like all of our lives we have been in this fantastic play Mark, with an amazing scene set, everything has been so good, perfectly acted out, but somehow you have given us the final curtain call, and it's all over, it's the end."

I started to shake as I spoke. I put my head into my hands to cover my eyes, as if I was trying to stop the steam of water, as the warm tears were running down my cheeks. I felt his arms around me as he cried too. Wound up in each other's arms and pain there didn't seem to be any answers. After what felt like forever sat on the stairs in our grief, Mark got up to leave.

"I am really sorry for everything Ruth. I really didn't want it to come to this."

I knew he meant it by the look in his eyes and the way he held my glance.

As he went out of the door he looked back at me again with his sad eyes. As if he knew that the life on the other side of the door wouldn't make him happy, but the life on my side of the door didn't make him happy either.

If only I had some magic solution to all of this, the way to make him want to be on this side again, in our normal lives and everything to go back to the way it had been.

Carol and Mark visit

It was Sunday afternoon. Having been horse riding and done my chores at the yard I had gone home, and was enjoying the warm afternoon sun, sat outside on the garden with the dogs.

I was on the phone to Kate. I was arranging to go and stay in Edinburgh with her for a few nights, and my trip was only a few days away. Kate had been telling me about all the best bars and restaurants and planning the sorts of things we might like to do whilst I stayed there. After our conversation I stretched out on the sun lounger, relaxing, looking forward to my week off work. The voices in my head were quiet, slightly cleared by yesterday's conversation with Mark. Seeing him so sad comforted me that he wasn't finding it easy ending our relationship either. It gave me part of the old Mark back.

My phone bing bonged to say I had got a message. It was Carol.

"Mark needs a few bits out of the garage so we are on our way over to see you." Followed by a Smiley face and kisses. I got up from the lounger and folded it into a chair shape. I started to pace up and down the back lawn, wondering what would happen. I didn't know how to feel about this. I was of course excited and about seeing Mark, as ever. It would be nice to see Carol too. I felt anxious though, no way of telling how conversations would go. I went back to sit in my comfy chair and tried to keep calm. I placed my sweaty palms in my lap and tried to hold them together to stop them shaking.

Carol and Mark arrived in his works van, I heard them pull up on the drive. I lay in the chair for a few seconds, fear and excitement not allowing me to move. Eventually I walked into the kitchen, Carol was already inside and came to greet me and put her arms around me. Mark was in the garage, I couldn't see him, but I could hear him banging about.

"I can't say too much, but quickly whilst he is out there, I have been having a good chat with him over the last few days and he is really missing you, I think he might want to come back" she said, staring into my eyes to gauge my response.

I looked at her in disbelief, I felt warm all over my body and my stomach did little flips, I was light headed and wobbly. Before we could say anything else to each other Mark strode into the kitchen.

"Hi Ruth, how are you today?" he looked right at me, warmly, like he actually cared, like a part of the old Mark was back in the kitchen with us. We all talked for a while, sipping cool drinks, and discussing my planned trip to Edinburgh and the dogs and what they have been up to and who has seen which relatives and are they all ok etc etc.

Carol was the first to make tracks to leave. "Well sorry, but we have got to go now, I need to go and visit my Dad and I promised we would be there over an hour ago."

"That's ok" I replied as I give her a hug and she smiled at me. Genuine and caring.

We were outside the garage by now and Mark was shutting the back of his van having put the last of the equipment he had collected inside.

He looked down at me and smiled as his mum got into the passenger seat.

I felt an electric feeling in the small space of air between us. We were close to each other and the tension was high. I could feel his breath on my face, and all I could think about was touching him, breaching the tiny gap between us.

"Catch you later shorty" he bent down and kissed me, gently on the lips. Of all the kisses we had ever shared, this was as good as any that had gone before it. My stomach did a complete somersault and I felt a buzz all over my body. For a few moments the world seemed to stand still whilst we just gazed into each other's eyes.

"Bye then" I said, stunned as he got into the driver's seat, shut the door, and slowly the van disappeared down the street. As they went off down the road I could see Carol raise a tissue to her face, obviously as shocked as I was and overcome with emotion.

Mark had just given me back a little piece of us and our memories, and more than that a little sliver of hope.

The day Mark came back

Mark and I usually took the last week in July off work, and we would usually also take the first week of August. We liked to try and get away for two weeks, somewhere warm, and have downtime, and celebrate our wedding anniversary.

I had already requested the time off work, long before Mark leaving me. Although we had not booked to go anywhere, and I could have changed it for another time, I decided to take it anyway, regardless of what Mark was doing. It didn't matter I needed the break and I was looking forward to a few days in Edinburgh, being pampered by my sister.

I had spent the first day off visiting my friend, Elizabeth, she and her husband lived about an hour away, in the city suburbs. It was my godson's birthday, and I had been to a specialist toy shop to get him a tractor, his latest obsession. On the drive to their house I could barely contain my excitement for the look on his face when he opened the gift. The tractor had the desired affect and Robert was ecstatic, he started making engine noises whilst pushing it up and down the lounge carpet.

Elizabeth had made cupcakes. They were delicious. Lots of pink and purple icing with sparkly baubles and stars on the top with pretty glitter. Although I had been struggling with my appetite Elizabeth's cakes broke through my emotionally driven hunger strike.

Whilst we munched on the delectable treats and chatted, it was nice to spend time together, just me and her, we could be open and honest whilst Robert played, happy to occupy himself, and I could take advantage of Elizabeth's frank advise.

My phone lit up. I had got a text message from Mark.

"Going to pick a mate up from the train station, don't know if you fancy a drive out?"

When family members or part of our social bubble needed dropping off or picking up then we would go together, glad of any reason to go for a drive, it was something we had done since we were young. It seemed normal him asking me, and after the kiss the day before, my stomach lurched over itself as I replied to his message.

"Sounds good, let me know what time I need to be ready?"

I told Elizabeth what he had put in the text. I had already told her everything else. Over the last two months Elizabeth and I had been in very close contact by text and phone and I had spent the last few hours filling in additional blanks.

"Do you think you will get back together now" she asked me thoughtfully. She was watching my response, I could feel her trying to read the thoughts in my head.

"I don't know, I really hope so, but it has to be what Mark wants" I tried to shrug it off, and make it sound like a small and insignificant decision, so that I didn't lay my emotions out too bare.

"Just be careful that it's actually what you want Ruth, that's all" Friends since school, she had always spoken her mind, and perhaps I should have paid more attention to her insightful words.

Making my excuses I needed to leave so I could go home and get ready to see Mark.

I hugged Elizabeth and Robert goodbye and headed off out of the city towards home.

When I get home I took the dogs out and thought about my dear friends words.

I wanted more than anything in the world to be back together with Mark. But I needed him to be happy, and I still didn't know how to do that, and I doubted whether he did either. Was it the strong woman's decision to stop what I was doing, like a puppet on a string, the moment he beckoned I was there. ….he needed a strong woman……I heard his words tick over ….you can never be what I want….I swallowed my fears down, took a deep breath and walked the trail……I could do this.

Once I was back home I changed into my favourite style, leggings and a long t shirt. Easy and slimming.I checked my hair, and added some more make-up. I wanted to make every best effort.

By the time I heard Marks car coming down the drive my heart felt liked it was in my mouth. I felt as if I could barely breathe, the anticipation of what might happen next felt like it was burning my lungs so no air could come in. He might kiss me again, or he might kill me again, I just couldn't know.

Mark strode into the house and made a fuss of the dogs whilst I got my shoes on and grabbed my handbag. Like we both normally would……

"Would you like to go and feed the horses and maybe then go for a burger or something?" Mark asked.

I was momentarily stunned by this olive branch. Firstly the offer of going to see the horses and then secondly going and getting something to eat.

"Yes please, that sounds great" was all I could manage in a surprised response.

We drove to the horse's yard in silence. It was a warm evening, Mark had his car stereo turned up loud, connected to the boom box and the beats of hard house echoed around us. The windows were all open and this caused a hot wind to rush through the car, blowing my hair out behind me. I snuggled down into the recaro racing seat as Mark pressed the accelerator. I never felt scared of high speeds when he was in control. I felt like we were both where we should be. I felt so alive.

Mark went into the horses field and checked them both over and stroked them whilst I got their feeds ready. He liked being around the horses, he was confident with them, their size not an issue to him; he was well within his comfort zone. I could tell from the stable yard though, that although he enjoyed being around Charlie, he was less patient with his thoroughbred ways, which were jumpy and sometimes flighty. With Lazer though it was love, I smiled to myself as I saw him carefully combing her forelock out of her eyes with his fingers. I had missed him being there. Missed sharing these wonderful animals with him.

Having fed the horses we both got back into the car and Mark drove towards the station. He closed all the windows and turns the air conditioning on; signalling he wanted to talk.

"Ruth, it feels wrong not being together. We are supposed to be together, I know we are. I have been thinking about you and me, and what makes me happy, and I just know that we can make this work, we should be together."

In every dream I had, since he left, Mark would say these words, and I fall into his arms and we would kiss and everything would be OK, all recent horror forgotten.

Now he was saying them for real I couldn't speak. My mouth wouldn't make sounds and my lips didn't seem to work. The moment I had prayed for had come, and I had become frozen in time.

"Is it what you want Ruth?" He half looked at me as he was driving along.

"Of course it is, you know it is" I smiled at him, finally able to speak.

A warm glow washed over me and I started to relax. We chatted enthusiastically all the way to the City, and all the way through our burgers about what we thought we may need to do to make our partnership succeed.

We only stopped when Marks friend got into the car for his lift. For a short period the three of us just made small talk about family and work. I didn't know how much Mark had told his friend, and kept to safe subjects. Once we had dropped him off at his house we could resume discussions.

Mark and I agreed that we would make lists of things that made us happy and things that we didn't want in our lives. We agreed we would both make our lists in secret, and then sit down together to look at them and agree on compromises where we wanted different things.

We also agreed that for the short term Mark would continue to live at his parents' house to give us some space from each other. I really wanted him to come home already, but he asked for the space for both of our sakes, saying that he didn't want to rush into things; he wanted them to be special.

It was such an odd feeling. When Mark left after all those years I didn't know what to say to him, how to handle the situation, but when he offered to come back I didn't know what to say then either.

Mark agreed that he would stay at the house and look after all the pets for me whilst I was in Edinburgh with my sister. He was happy to stay at the house if I wasn't there, he felt there would be no pressure and was looking forward to spending some time with the dogs.

By the time we had finished talking it was nearly mid night. Sat at the bottom the stairs we were like two teenagers. I looked in to his eyes and I felt he really wanted it. Us. Me. We kissed each other, and the old passion was there. So much so I was almost afraid of my feelings. There was an immense, new energy.

"I'm going now Ruth, it doesn't feel right that this goes any further" he smiled and looked down at me as he stood.

"I really want to make this work, and I just hope that one day you will be able to forgive me. I hope you can forgive me for what I did to you."

As the Evo bumbled off loudly down the street his words went over again in my thoughts.

Forgive him. I think I knew the truth as I stood in the dark in the hallway. I didn't think I could ever fully forgive him, but I was going to put all of my efforts into trying

Edinburgh and back

The morning after I woke, and my world couldn't have been more different from the one I had been living in for the previous few months. I had the relaxed and warm feeling that Mark and I were back together, coupled with the excitement that I was going to Edinburgh.

Mark had decided to take the morning off work and drive me to the railway station. At the station he walked me to the platform. I had a small suitcase and everything I needed for a few nights away. Mark said goodbye and we kissed on the platform. I looked up in to his soft, kind eyes. And he beamed. I felt like I was back in a safe place. Like the old Mark was back.

Once Mark was gone from the platform I realised I was a little early for my train, so I wondered up to the café, and got a tall, cold mocha and a large chocolate cake. My appetite was back and I felt ravenous. I sat back on the platform and devoured the sugary treats, daydreaming away as I chewed.

Once I was on the train I got my notebook out. I had a task. I needed to write my list.

As I put pen to paper, I began to realise that, unlike the long list of issues Mark had given in the recent weeks, my only real gripe was that we didn't seem to make more time for each other.

I pondered further, and supposed that as I hadn't seen all of the trouble coming, maybe I didn't get time to consider what I didn't like about our relationship. Was that was mainly because I had been content? Or had I simply not thought about re-designing the portfolio of us...

I recall being unsure what to state as ' wrong'. I decided that instead I would think of a list of the things that made me happy, perhaps that would draw me to a conclusion.

Having had the dogs to myself for the first time ever, I had realised how important it was to me that I was a part of their daily exercise routine, and I couldn't see why we shouldn't be walking them together in the evenings. I wrote that down.

I also wanted us to make more of an effort to spend time together away from the house and away from the pets. Go out for dinner or to the cinema. Maybe go away for weekends like we had when we were younger. I added that to the list.

Having a really honest moment I thought I should add that I wasn't really ready to have children at the time, but that this didn't mean I never wanted them. I thought it was only fair that I should be very clear on that.

As the train shook gently from side to side I looked out of the windows as green countryside rolled by. I started to think further into the things that Mark wanted. Some of the compromises that he might want me to make, and perhaps concessions I should be thinking about making anyway.

I added to the list that perhaps we should consider downsizing to a smaller house to release some money, but even as I wrote it I couldn't bear the thought of leaving our home. I realised how important the seeming lack of money had become to Mark, and he was correct that a lot of our finances were committed to just bricks and mortar. But I hoped he would never make us leave.

There was a bigger compromise I knew I needed to make. Having two horses and working full time was difficult. Especially as they both needed riding and the investment of time. Charlie and Lazer were like chalk and cheese. She was young, dominant and demanding. I had owned her since she was weaned. Charlie was older, wiser, but distrustful and very quick to escape from any human pressure. He was probably more dangerous to me because I lacked the experience needed to deal with him. Maybe I could consider getting someone to the yard who might want to share him, or maybe there was someone out there who would like to take him on? As I wrote the words though it felt like I was giving up on Charlie. But I needed to do this if I wasn't going to give up on Mark.

The journey was mostly taken up by the list, and towards the latter part, watching nervously for the correct stop, I was both tired and relieved by the time the train got into the station.

I was pleased to see Kate's boyfriend Charles waiting for me and he gave me a warm hug and popped my luggage into the back of his car.

"Kate is still at work, so we are going to the pub for a while." Charles smiled, pleased with his decision. I agreed that this was an excellent idea.

I loved being in Edinburgh. The bars and restaurants and the way I can walk down the street to get dinner, it's a far cry from living out in the sticks as I always have. Amusing that Kate and I were brought up in the same way but chose very different lifestyles, and although I am no city slicker I do enjoy joining in with the cosmopolitan feel whenever I stay with her.

I relaxed in the bar with the tall glace of white wine Charles had bought me.

Kate walked into the bar. But I knew it was her as she came down the street and I could see her out of the thick glass windows. We walk the same. Not really a graceful walk, more of a purposeful stomp, braced to move other people out of the way. I watched her march along with love and fondness.

Kate came in and I jumped up and hugged her and kissed her. It felt so good to be in each others arms.

"Ruth you look very skinny!" I felt as if I was being scolded, my younger sister always wiser than I. "Charles and I will have to feed you up."

The break I had in Edinburgh with Kate and Charles was just what I needed. They did feed me well. They took me to amazing bistros and places off the beaten track, their local knowledge meant we were in really good locations but they were never busy.

They treated me to a ghost walk one night. I think we were supposed to be scared in a pitch black area under the main city, but we weren't, we just laughed and joked about it. A little woman whispering to us in candlelight with her face part covered by a scarf, and we were several stories below ground, in old stone ruins. Kate got the giggles, Charles told a fart joke. That's was it, hysterics ensued, much to the disapproval of those around us.

When the ghost tour had finished we came out of the dark to find a party in the streets and grown men seeing how fast they could go downhill, bobbling along on the cobbles on their bicycles. We were unable to avoid staring at them and their drunken antics. We stopped and watched for a while as they piled up against a wall at the bottom of the hill in various stages of injury.

Charles and Kate were also very patient with my love of arts and tolerated several visits to galleries, with coffee shop and wine bar visits in between. We also spent another day cycling to the beach.

The break away from the house, the pets and Mark made the voices in my head stop, the cold shivery feeling left me alone and I felt free of any emotional ties. Even if it were just for a few days it was bliss.

Charles and Kate were especially good at distracting me on the thirtieth of July. It was our fifth wedding anniversary. The ways things had been left between Mark and I made me wonder if we were celebrating or not. I felt confused.

In the morning Mark had sent me a text saying "don't think I don't know what day it is and I am thinking about it." This had brought tears to my eyes as I remembered the happy times of our special day.

Mark and I had broken tradition and decided it didn't matter if we saw each other on our wedding morning. We had gone to a water park with Jack, Kit and Kate. We played on the flumes and ate pizza and drank beer. At about 4pm Dad had been sent as the nominated person to collect the wedding party to go and prepare for the evening ceremony. He has forgotten that was what he was supposed to be doing and ended up staying and having one too many drinks.

Kate and I laughed about this as we recalled the happy day whist walking around the pretty Edinburgh streets and shops. In a card shop I was poised over the anniversary cards.

"I don't know what to do Kate? I don't know if I should get one or not?" I felt really muddled as I looked to her for advise.

"Look at them all Ruth, they all say happy anniversary across them, and you haven't been having a happy time lately. I would just wait and see how you feel when you get back."

I knew she was right. But I bought one anyway and hid it in my suitcase, in fear that maybe Mark would get me one, and I would feel awful if I didn't reciprocate. I need not have worried.

The day after Kate and Charles put me back on the train and we all said our good byes. I felt sad as I waved back at them as the train pulled out of the station. But I looked forward to coming back for the New Year.

Back on familiar turf, Mark picked me up from the station. I hopped off the train and onto the platform, feeling warm and relaxed. I wheeled my trolley suitcase nosily over the bridge and around to the car park and got into his van next to him. We smiled at each other. How I had missed this closeness. When we have been away from each other for a few days and didn't get to talk properly, and then when we saw each other again, how good it felt. We kissed. Our mouths on each others and a heady mix of emotions and excitement, my stomach full of butterflies.

Mark drove me home. We had some tea together and sat on the sofa to watch the telly.

All the passion got the better of us, and it was as tender as it had ever been, Mark taking me to places that nobody else ever had before him. We were as one again. We made our way to bed and slept for the first time in weeks, together in the same bed, our marital bed, in our room. In the morning we made love again. Mark rolled onto this side and looked at me, the old fondness there in his eyes. " Ruth it's like we are teenagers again, it feels so good."

After a while we got up and went to sit in the office bedroom. Both with a coffee in our hands, we were eager to see each other lists. It was curious. We had both said that we were neither of us ready to have children yet. Marks list said that he was worried Lazer would hurt me for real one day, and I needed some professional help, and he had also written that Charlie should have another home. My heart slowed as I read that part. I knew it would be there but I still hated seeing it. Mark said that we should be going on more days out together, and we were overdue a holiday.

Marks usual sense of humour seemed to have returned as well, because part of his list said that my horse doesn't complain if I ride other horses, so he should be able to ride other women!

As we read through the lists it appeared there were no big surprises and we seemed to pretty much be in agreement on paper.

I put feelers out with the my horsy connections, Charlie would be the first item on my list, as I demonstrated my commitment to Mark, by showing him I could face the biggest challenge he had requested. I would do this to earn back his love and respect; no matter how hard it hurt.

We spent the rest of the day mooching. Mostly we just sat in each other's arms. The togetherness felt so good, and so right.

All that was left was for us to start to implement some of the things we had detailed. Some would come faster than others, and some would never come at all.

The day I let Charlie go

It was September. Mark and I had been back together for a couple of weeks.

Things felt almost normal. There had been some half awkward conversations with relatives and friends, mostly concerned, some just being nosey and wishing to stir up trouble. But all who were close to us were as happy as we were.

We had both made more of an effort to go out for days together, we had spent every Sunday in each other's company, and we had been out for dinner more too. We had an arrangement where I slept in the main bedroom and Mark slept in the spare room. It was by mutual agreement since Mark had come back to the house, and as neither of us had wanted to rush things, we had both opted for a little space. It was a compromise from him always being at his parents house.

It had certainly spiced things up a bit. It was exciting to wait until both bedroom lights were out and then tip toe across the landing to each other's rooms like naughty teenagers creeping around in their parents' house. It was fun and had interjected plenty of passion.

The day had come when Charlie would be going to his new home. I had been contacted by a friend of a friend who was interested in having Charlie. She has been to see him. She was a riding instructor, her attitude was fair, but firm, and from having met her she was clearly experienced. Carla said that Charlie seemed calm to her, she worked with a lot of racehorses, and ex racehorses, and she thought he would make a nice quiet hack.

I was satisfied that letting Carla have Charlie would be the best option all round. It would pacify Mark, give me more time to work with Lazer, and give Charlie to a home with the experience he deserved.

But mostly it was about pacifying Mark. I needed to try and be the person he wanted me to be. I needed to try and give up my inner needs to take in every injured and needy animal and nurse it back to life. From what we had both agreed about spending less on things two horses was a luxury we could not afford. I was stuck between who I was and who I needed to be.

Carla came to collect Charlie and we had agreed that if she could load him, we would transport him in our trailer. Loading Charlie was difficult and stressful. He didn't want to go in the trailer. He became like a dragon, with his orange nostrils flared up snorting as if ready to breathe fire, and sweat dripped out of him. As I sat on the stone yard watching Carla eventually load him into the trailer and shut the back door my heart sunk to my stomach. I had failed Charlie. I had accepted him because he needed a home and Lazer needed a friend and but then I was allowing him to be taken away.

Lazer and Charlie whinnied and squealed to each other, she was galloping up and down the field; he was banging the front of the trailer with his neatly shod little hooves.

Mark drove us all to Charlie's new home slowly and carefully. We watched as he ran into a paddock to join his new friends and play. His beautiful chestnut fur a blur as his athletic frame moved at speed with the other horses.

He barely noticed when we left, so for all the failure I felt from the top of my head to the tip of my toes I don't think he held it against me.

I didn't accept any money for Charlie. I even gave Carla the expensive rugs I had bought for him. I felt he was entitled to them.

Mark and I drove back to our yard in silence. When we got there I had visions in my head of Lazer with a broken leg, where she had tried to jump the fence to follow her friend, or garrotted herself on barbed wire, or lying down ill on the ground. As we got around the corner of barn she was none of those things. She was grazing away swishing her tail without a care in the world. Just like Charlie she had accepted the human decisions. The ease of living in that moment. I still envy that now.

The only person judging me for this was me.

We got back to the house and I didn't really know what to say to Mark and I don't think he knew what to say to me. As we walked down the familiar trail with the dogs running happily around us I looked down at the sandy path and no words would come. Just a heavy feeling in the pit of my stomach.

We went to bed, to our own separate rooms. We each pulled our bedroom doors shut and turned off our lights.

At last, once I was in the dark I felt I could stop pretending I was OK. I could wipe the brave smile off my face. I sat on the thick pile black carpet, with my back to the leather on the side of the bed. I pulled my knee's up and put my head on them. I let the silent tears fall, washing down my face and dripping on to my legs.

I had failed on my journey, to give a horse a home that needed one. I had failed on my journey to ride my mare properly too, as my back creaked and ached from the fall I had from her. The dreams I had of being a horsewoman had been taken from me by my own inability. Meanwhile I needed comfort from my husband and partner, who was in the next room, but may as well have been a thousand miles away.

"Ruth, are you OK?" Mark asked through the shadows from his room.

"Yes, I think so" I lied, as I answered him.

He knew it was a lie, and I knew he knew it was a lie. That's the difficulty of knowing someone all those years. You can pretend all you like, but they know your true feelings even better than you do yourself at times. I sat there knowing he asked me because he felt guilty.

We just had to both hope that these sacrifices were for the greater good. But at that place in time Mark wouldn't go the extra mile from his room and comfort me. And I wouldn't admit that I need help and sympathy and let my barriers down.

Rebecca

Eventually we moved back into the same bedroom, and I think we were starting to put a little more trust in each other.

We were friends again, we alternated between walking the dogs together in the evenings, and him taking them alone whilst I would spend more time with Lazer and admittedly with only one horse I did have more time.

We were heading towards winter time, the evenings were drawing in and the weather was starting to feel colder, leaving more time for cuddling in front of the fire in the evenings. An image painted in the mind of an idealist. Perhaps a cream front room, with wine on the table as lovers embrace, their passion as warm as the flames. We began the slow struggle, to return to a level of normality. I can only tell you how I wanted it to feel in my head, because I will honestly never know how it felt in Marks.

One evening he came home and told me that he had been to look at a small job our village, just around the corner. I recalled how we had been to look at houses on that estate, it backed onto ours, I could remember the buildings were similar brickwork and quality, but we rejected the estate, the rooms were small and so were the gardens….not really relevant and I was only half listening.

The chap whose house it was happened to be out at work when Mark went to the house to look at the job, and price up for it, so he had been let in and showed around by the chaps girlfriend. I was nodding and smiling, but I was also wondering about what we might watch on the telly, or could we get a takeaway for tea…..

For some reason she had managed to tell him that their relationship was not a happy one, there were stories of fights, assault and arguments, even him kicking her out. Not asking her to leave, removing her from what I now understood to be his house. I thought that level of confidentiality was high in someone you had only just met. Why would they be exchanging that level of conversation…

As Mark was telling me all about this woman, the cold feeling started to slowly creep all over me. A light of anxiety switched on inside my head. Unseen to Mark I am sure, but he now had my undivided attention. It was the first time I had felt that like in a month or so and it was not a welcome return. Something was just really odd and uncomfortable about what he was telling me.

"Did you tell her about us Mark? About our problems and what we had to do about them?" I needed to ask him. I knew in the pit of my stomach that if this woman had been so open and honest with Mark, then there was a high chance he had reciprocated.

"Yes Ruth, I did" He was calm, looking at me in an unusual way, was this some sort of a confession?

I wasn't comfortable with how this situation was unfolding, my mouth was dry and I felt cold all over, a strange prickly sensation was running up both of my arms.

How odd that you should meet someone for the first time, whilst supposedly looking at their house to complete electrical work in a professional capacity, and instead you should find yourself sharing personal traumas, and divulging you own. Strange unless there was some sort of a bond. Attraction? And more poignantly, why come home and tell me about it? I felt puzzled and uneasy. The voices began to chitter chatter at me. I willed them away , to no avail, everyone's words on repeat.

Mark built up a friendship with Rebecca, and over the next few days they became friends on social media, and started texting each other.

I explained to Mark that I was not happy. But he seemed to ignore my sentiments. Maybe he just hoped I would leave him to it.

Within a day or two of our initial conversation about Rebecca I sneaked a look at her through Marks profile. She looked pretty and slim, with dark hair and piercing blue green eyes. I knew then as I stared at the screen she was every bit of everything that I wasn't. She had piercings all over her body and wore dark make-up, maybe slightly gothic. Certainly very sexualized. I knew that to Mark she would seem exciting. Irresistible?

My feelings of unease grew for about a week after the conversation and then oddly, Mark stopped mentioning her, as if his interest in her had come and gone as quickly as the job that had then been completed at the house she was living in. I made a mental note to close the door on the thoughts I had about their friendship.

It was another couple of weeks later when eventually Rebecca's relationship broke down so badly with the man she was living with that she moved out. And went back to her family, miles away. I knew all about it because Mark kept coming home and telling me what was going on again.

That she had been asked to leave her house. When she was leaving. How awful her ex-partner was to her. How the police seemed to be involved. And that she had to go and live quite a distance away and mostly how Mark seemed to be very worried about her.

I wanted to believe that they were just friends. But I think in a place I wasn't prepared to uncover at that time, I feared this was something to worry about and the truth should stay locked away for a while longer. And I went back to pretending that all was perfectly normal and OK, back in the cream lounge with the wine, in front of the fire.

Matlock and Eggs

It was a Sunday morning and Mark and I had travelled to the Derbyshire hills, to one of our favourite spots. A beautiful village with lots of ice cream parlours, bistro's and gift shops. Just me, him and the dogs. It was a place we had always gone, since we were teenagers.

We were sat in my truck, enjoying gourmet burgers and coffee we had picked up along the way.

We were well into November and it was a cold and rainy day outside, we were glad to be sat inside the shelter of the vehicle, consuming sustenance to prepare for the cold blast, we would feel when we braved the outdoors.

I sat and watched the rain drops making trickles down the windscreen, they gathered together to make streams as they then turned into small waterfalls.

Marks phone made constant noises and vibrations as he got text messages and updates. Some of them he relayed to me, others he did not. He mentioned that we were near to where Rebecca was living now, maybe she would like to join us? I didn't relish that as an option. Another girl who was always chasing after him, Sally, also kept messaging him and said that she wished she was with him. I could see that he blatantly enjoyed the attention, and the interest flattered him. Why I needed to be updated remained a mystery.

But as we sat in the truck eating the food I felt sad. I wished that there was just one day in time when I was enough for Mark. Couldn't there just be time for us? Where he turned off his phone and paid attention to only me, and shut down his harem of admirers?

I thought back to not so long ago when I would have his undivided attention, we would talk and laugh and play and the time was our own. But that place was gone. I had to share him with whomever wanted a piece.

I looked at myself in the wing mirror. If I was slimmer, or prettier or cleverer ? If I wore better clothes? Maybe if we had more similar interests? Or perhaps less? I blinked back the tears and swallowed the cold feeling with my warm drink, as it threatened to come up through my throat take over my body. I realised that never again would I be enough for Mark. He needed more than I could ever give him. I silently figured that it was better to share someone than to not have them in your life at all.

It was like closing a drawer and locking my fears away in it.

Later on when we were home for the evening we had the fire on in the lounge, and the dogs were sprawled out in front of it. Outside the rain had started to turn to snow.

Mark and I were rummaging around in the kitchen, to see what we could rustle up for tea.

"I'm going out to the shop to get some Eggs' Mark stated' They will help me build muscle."

Ever since Mark and I had been back together he had been maintaining a very detailed fitness routine, with a treadmill and a full set of weights in the garage. He had become larger, heavier and more muscular than ever, and having always prided himself in his physique, his quest for the perfect body was becoming more intense.

He would spend hours in his home made garage gym, red faced, staring at himself in the mirror, pushing himself to the limits, and dripping with sweat.

I agreed with him about the Eggs. But there was one strange thing. Mark didn't like Eggs and never had. He was repulsed by them. He wasn't even able to swallow a small mouthful of white.

"But you don't like Eggs" I laughed.

Mark was already in the hallway, wrapping up in his coat, hat and gloves.

"Well, I am going to make myself like them. I will have them as a drink with milk, or perhaps as an omelette."

And off he went.

Sometime after we had eaten our eggs (I had watched his face contort whilst he forced them down) Mark was in the garage lifting weights. He had house music booming and the noise leaked upstairs. I was sat on the spare bed alone, my hackles prickled.

Something was wrong. I didn't know what it was. It wasn't something I could describe, and in fact I think I probably still cant. Just a creepy feeling. The realisation I had felt that morning over Marks steady stream of admirers. How I really couldn't be what he wanted. And now he had become training and fitness obsessed and was forcing himself to like a food that he had always hated.

But that was all it was. Just a collection of facts. I didn't want to ponder them anymore. Closing the mental drawer again I went back downstairs to watch the TV.

My 30th Birthday

The snow that had fallen at the end of November signalled the start of a long and very cold snap. We saw the deepest snow we had experienced in years, so bad that villages were cut off from civilisation, and for a few days I was unable to get to work at the office, even in my 4 x 4. Temperatures plummeted to minus 17 at times, and the countryside spent weeks covered in a white blanket.

When Mark and I woke on the 2nd of December it was my 30th birthday. I could tell by the bright white of the room as I woke that we had more snow overnight. Even with the curtains drawn it was reflecting, and the light was breaking into the room. I opened the curtains, shocked and surprised but excited.

"Oh my god Mark look! We have had even more for my birthday" I squealed like an excited child.

The snow was up to the bottom of both vehicles on the drive, and had blown like a blizzard up the side of the horse trailer, it was barely recognisable.

We got up and got dressed and went downstairs. I opened the patio door in the dining room to let the dogs out to the toilet, and I was shocked as I slid the door open, a foot of snow fell in, an indication of how deep it was, as the door was already several inches off the ground.

Mark and I sipped our coffees and laughed , watching Mia go out first, into the snow, which came to the top of her back, we could only see her ears and her nose, and this cut a path for the slightly smaller Phoenix, who we could barely see at all. Pharaoh cat followed them, but she could only make any progress by launching up through the air, out of the snow, and making big white holes where she had landed. They all came back inside and shook the cold white flakes off themselves.

We went to the stable yard together, the truck catching every few yards as the deep snow touched the bottom of it, it was a struggle but we made it up the lane eventually.

We watched quietly as the dogs and horse frolicked in the sparkely landscape around us. I am always amused at how much my equine buddies like to roll around in snow, whilst Lazer enjoyed herself I made her stable up and then brought her in again. Mark would normally accuse me of being too soft on her, but this time he agreed that she may injure herself struggling with such deep snow. Lazer was perfectly happy back in the stable munching on hay.

When we got home we got changed out of our dirty, wet clothes and I sat on the edge of our bed in my underwear wondering what to wear on account of our new climate.

"What would you like to do today Ruth? It is your Birthday after all?" Mark asked me.

"I just don't know" I called across to Mark who was sat at the computer chair in the office "I would love to go out somewhere but I think we may really battle to get to anywhere that is even open in this weather" I was a little disappointed really. Mark and I had booked my Birthday off so we could spend some time together, and although I loved snow, I hadn't expected this volume.

He came into our bedroom and sat on the edge of the black leather next to me and pulled me on to his knee.

I turned to face him and looked into his eyes. They looked sad.

"What's the matter? Are you upset about the weather?" I asked him

"No, I just wanted to do something really good for your birthday , to treat you, you know, but now I think we won't be able to go anywhere or do anything. I even wonder if we will be able to get to the restaurant for tea" he looked a bit forlorn, his brow in a frown, puzzling "I had really wanted to take you somewhere special. I wanted to take you to New York you know….we could go to bars and restaurants and hang out in Time Square, a place I really knew you would love, for your special Birthday." his eyes were shiny with tears now. Still holding me in his arms, strong and steady, but he had a defeated look about him.

'Why didn't you do it then?' I asked gently and curiously

"I was worried that we couldn't really afford it Ruth that we didn't have the money, I should have just got on with it, but I haven't and now we are doing nothing."

When I looked at Mark that morning I realised that his changed behaviour had arrived in a new dimension. He had become depressed. And feeling as if he was letting me down and disappointing me added a bigger burden to him. My heart sank as I sat in his arms, I just didn't know how to help him.

"Well we are going to the Angel for tea aren't we, I love it there" I smiled at him. "Let's get dressed again and take the dogs down the trail, it will be fun."

I was wrong about it being fun. Due to the extreme conditions everyone was off work and all the schools were shut. The trail was full of lots of children running along with sledges, and they all seemed to be worried or nervous about two bouncy dogs. We walked on over a snow covered field and away from the busy areas, until there was just us. The sky was black almost. Full of more snow. And it came down in enormous flakes, falling slowly and silently at first, but it wasn't long before Mark and I were battling against a blizzard and even the dogs looked miserable. We held hands, Mark almost pulling me through snow that came up past the top of my boots. It was up to my knees. My back had started aching because of the angles I was having to walk at, and as we started back towards home it became excruciating.

"Come on Ruth, you can make it" he laughed, and then said quietly "see, this is why we don't go walking together, you just go too slowly."

We did eventually make it back and decided to get changed into our going out clothes before checking on Lazer again.

I dressed in jeans and a sparkly top. We had both been to the restaurant before, and I knew that it had an upmarket, country chic vibe, and I needed to look my best.

Mark drove us along the challenging windy roads. They were only slightly clearer than they had been in the morning; whatever ploughing had been done earlier had since been covered by new snow, which was still coming hard and fast.

I felt happy that Mark was at the steering wheel, he was a more confident and experienced driver than I was, and he was also happy to play in the snow, insisting he knew a shortcut and power sliding the truck sideways along treacherous back roads.

I was spoiled to a lavish three course meal, one of my favourite things was venison with chocolate sauce. And some champagne which was brought out by the waiter in a fancy ice bucket.

Mark had always spoiled me and he wasn't about to stop now.

But there was one difference.

It was Marks mobile phone. He wouldn't let it out of his sight. It was always right next to one of his hands, usually the right. And it made quiet beeps, or flashed constantly, literally every few moments. Sometimes he would update as to who he was chatting to, and include me in their conversations, if it was someone I knew then it would almost become a three way text chat. Other times he was silent and pensive and I didn't know who he was in conversation with.

This had become the pattern at home of an evening, or if we were sat watching the telly, just the same as when we had gone out for the day. And now it was the same in the restaurant. Even on this, my Birthday, I wasn't enough for him. As we sat facing each other eating our dinner and chatting I felt as if Mark may as well have been talking to every other person in the restaurant as he split his chatter between me and his virtual friends. And I felt ever so slightly, just a prickle of the cold feeling creeping over me. Just a few hairs on my neck stood on end, just a bit more liqueur coffee needed to dampen my drying mouth, but it was there. The sensation that I was not enough for Mark, and he needed to fill in where I was lacking, with other people.

But I gulped down and buried the feeling back inside myself. Locking the thoughts away in the drawer again.

The 30th Birthday Family Meal

The following day we had planned that we would go our local pub for tea. A second birthday celebration.

It would be the first time everyone was going to be together in a long while, Mark and I would feel the support of the two sides of our families.

I had spoken to Kate on my birthday. Her and Charles wouldn't make it down from Scotland, but that was understandable. Their snow was so bad that they could not even find their cars, buried in drifts up to six foot high.

Mark and I were getting ready when the home phone rang. He was in the bath, and I was stood with some towels on my head and around my body, so I dashed to pick up .It was mum.

"I'm really sorry Ruth, we aren't coming" she sounded very adamant.

"Why aren't you coming?" I said disappointed and surprised

"Because of the snow. Last night it turned to black ice up here, and your Dad has already bumped his car on the lane and we don't want to risk it gain, especially in the dark."

"I can understand what you are saying Mum, but the main roads aren't actually that bad you know. It's only some of the side roads, I guess that's why Dad had such trouble on your little lane. But the pub car park and the roads around it are fine, we have been to check."

"We are just not prepared to risk it, I'm sorry, can we arrange to do it another time?"

"Of course we can't" I was shouting, unable to hide my anger, and I knew Mum would be able to hear it in my voice but I didn't care.

"We can't just re-organise my Birthday, and everyone else is already coming, Marks parents are already on the way, we have started getting ready, I can hardly call it all off."

I hung up furiously. Why were they letting me down like this. It wasn't just about my Birthday. It was about unity, having everyone together, being normal. Mark had heard the whole story from the bathroom.

"I knew they would do this Ruth. I just knew it. Why the hell do they live off down those country roads and not have a 4x4 by now. It happens all the time. I can't believe it." He was fuming. And it was making me feel anxious all the more.

"Call them back, tell them they can all stay over there is plenty of room?" this made good sense. I was about to pick up the phone and dial, but it was already ringing in my hand and surprised me.

It was my brother Jack.

"Hey dude, Mum says you are not coming because of the snow, I am gutted so Mark says why don't you just all stay over?"

Jack went to ask Mum and Dad about this, I could hear him making it sound like an appealing option with all of his usually enthusiasm. He came back to the phone.

"It's still a no isn't it?" I asked sensing the answer and feeling upset.

"Fraid so, but anyway me and Rachel and Kit are still coming, we have told Mum and Dad we don't care, we are walking to the bus stop, can you pick us up at the other end?"

"Sure, course we can" I smiled. At least my brothers weren't going to let me down. And Jack was even brining his girlfriend along for the fun.

Jack, Kit and Rachel got to Mansfield bus station to discover that there would be no more buses, other than to a village a few miles away, so Jack quickly made the decision that they would take that bus and get as far as they could under their own steam and called Mark and I to go and collect them from that point.

Once we had collected them we drove straight to the pub, all laughing and joking as one of the trucks windscreen wipers gave in against the harsh weather and disappeared. We slid around on the roads, only able to see out of one side of the car, not the driver's side, and so all the passengers were hung out of various windows issuing directions to Mark who drove commendably.

I felt embarrassed when Carol and Patrick asked where Mum and Dad were. They said that they would have gone and got them.

"Don't worry, we tried everything" Mark spat. "They just couldn't be arsed."

"Yeah we managed to make it through!" Jack said, clearly he wasn't happy with my parents actions either. The atmosphere turned uncomfortable as we all sat around the table. Mark was getting aggressive and confrontational, and nobody seemed to have a good word to say. Joanna, bright as ever , shot me a friendly look across the table, and said brightly, "Ruth, why don't you start opening cards and presents" for which I was grateful for.

Many drinks and some delicious steaks later we said our goodbyes to Carol and Patrick and Martyn and Joanna, and the rest of us made our way up the street back home slipping and sliding as we went. We left the truck at the pub, Mark and I were too drunk to consider driving, and it was doubtful it would go anywhere in those conditions.

Back home Mark cracked open the spirits. We all sat and watched a horror film. Rachel and I clung to each other. Jack and Kit joked about how the movie wasn't that scary.

After a short while Mark got up off the sofa and stomped out of the room, saying simply "I'm going to bed." He had removed himself from the jolly atmosphere, for reasons I couldn't fathom.

"Is he OK do you think?" Jack asked quietly "Course he isn't" Kit replied "he is still pissed off with mum and Dad." "Nah, that's not it" I added "there is something else, I don't know what it is, but there is something, he just doesn't seem himself."

"He doesn't say much anymore does he? And when he does, it's angry" Jack pondered

"And he never leaves his phone alone either" Rachel commented quietly, so she had noticed. I felt assurances that I wasn't alone in my observations, or that it was unusual.

I had spent all evening trying to pretend that the atmosphere wasn't there. That everything was normal, when I knew it wasn't, and my younger siblings had noticed it all by themselves.

Baffling behaviour

The following day Marks behaviour continued to baffle me.

I thought he would forgive my parents for not coming the night before. Whilst I didn't agree with their actions, things were as they were, so I felt we had choice but to accept them.

When Mum and Dad offered to come and pick up my brothers and bring me a Birthday cake, although it was a little late I agreed.

I arranged to meet them at the yard. I needed to spend some time clearing snow, making up haynets and preparing the stable. Hard winter weather can be cruel to horse owners, but I didn't mind being out in the cold, so long as I was wrapped up warm. I knew Rachel would like to see Lazer too, as a fellow horse lover.

No amount of persuasion would make Mark join us. His head bowed low, in argument, no, he was adamant that he wasn't coming with us to the yard and he didn't want to see my parents. When I tried to press him on it he just got angrier and I didn't want to make him explode in front of my brothers. So I drove over to the yard reluctantly and Mark got left behind at the house alone.

At the time it never occurred to me that perhaps Mark had another agenda, maybe there was another reason he didn't want to join us, and the disagreement with my parents was making a useful excuse?

Although the main roads had been cleared, thick snow still billowed out into the fields and the landscape was hidden under a deep white blanket. Icicles hung under all of the stable eves, sparkling in the last of the daylight. Dad helped me pack up some hay nets under the shelter of the barn. We laughed at how impossible it was with thick gloves on, but how unbearably icy the wind was if we dared to take our fingers out of the woollen protection. Mum managed to light some candles on a cake she had made, and they all sang to me. What an amusing picture, my family huddled around each other singing happy birthday outside my horses stable, whist she munched on her hay and looked on in curiosity.

Mark was conspicuous by his absence. Mum kept asking me about it. "Where is Mark?" or "Is he OK Ruth?" or "What did he get you for your birthday?."

What could I say? He is really mad with you for not coming last night for dinner and for some reason he is not coming here now either in some sort of bizarre retaliation. But I kept the response within myself. The truth she would not find palatable, but as I shrugged it off to my parents I looked at Jack and Kit. They knew the same as I did. That probably wasn't even why he wasn't with us. There was another reason why he hadn't come and joined in with the festivities. It's just that none of us knew what it was. Maybe even Mark himself didn't know……

The Day of the Truck Argument

After weeks of extremely low temperatures and very deep snow, we finally got some respite.

Mark and I planned to head into town to buy some Christmas gifts for family, and then he had a tattoo session booked.

When Mark and I were first together he had disapproved of body art, like piercings and ink on skin, where as I had always been very interested in such adornment, even doing a college project on the subject towards my A Level Art exam. Mark had shown little interest, and had been disgusted when I had gone to a tattoo parlour for the day with my friend.

Years later when Mark had been diagnosed with his diabetes he changed his mind set completely. I designed him a dragon tattoo, which he had etched on to his back in black work. Over the following years he had more, larger pieces all over his arms and torso, and going for these tattoo sittings was something he now loved. I guessed it went with his training obsession. Appearances mattered. The decorated body beautiful.

As we drove together into town to there was a busy bustling everywhere. Mark became irritated by the lack of parking spaces, and I could feel the tension rise between us. I felt scared that we were heading towards one of our rows. I suggested that we go to get some coffee and calm down.

Even the drive through was rammed. There was nowhere to go. Cars queuing like dominoes at every entrance and exit.

"Never mind Mark, forget it, I will get coffee later" I felt myself prickle as I pretended we should give up.

"But Ruth you made me drive back up to other side of town to get coffee and now you don't want one!" he exclaimed, angrily. "Well yes I do want one, but I can't see where we can park, and I can tell that you are getting mad so maybe we should just get out of here."

"Oh for Gods sake Ruth you will make up your mind one day!" he spat at me, and the truck lurched forwards as he forced his way through the traffic.

Something inside of me snapped. I couldn't put up with another one of his temper tantrums. Why could he never stay calm? I leapt out of the truck and slammed the passenger door shut. "Screw you Mark."

I walked off up the road that led out of town. Its miles away from the village that we lived in, but I didn't care. I wasn't thinking logically. I felt boiling hot, and furious, I just needed to be away from Mark, I couldn't carry on with this anymore. He was going from sullen and sad, to angry and stroppy at the drop of a hat. I thought I was going mad, it must be me that was making him behave like that, I believed as I stomped heavily along the footpath that heads out of town.

Even in the chilly wind I was hot, I went along the pavement briskly, head down and my jumper tied around my waist, considering what I should do next.

I knew that Mark would have driven off home. The further I walked the more I regretted my reactions. I should not have met fire with fire.

In our younger years if I had flown off in anger to escape an argument, Mark would follow me, but I knew he wouldn't follow me anymore. I had lost that appeal. The further I walked the more I started to slow. My back was beginning to hurt and I realised my feet were blistered. As I had jumped out of the truck I had left my phone and purse behind. I had no money and no way of communicating with Mark, or anyone else for that matter. This had been a mistake on my part. I had chosen the right time to make a stand, but the wrong way in which to do it.

Finally I arrived at a village a few miles away from the one we lived in. I was aching, and emotional, but I needed to try and catch Mark before he left to go to the tattoo sitting. Perhaps we could still go together, and I could rescue the rest of the day.

Having no further options I began to walk past houses on the main road and stare in to see if anyone was at home. I was going to have to ask to use a phone. The first few doors I knocked on there was no answer.

By the time I got to the third one I was beginning to cry, ashamed of my behaviour, and embarrassed that I would have to ask to use a phone like this. I knocked anyway. An older man opened the door.

"I'm really sorry, I have had an argument with my husband, and left my phone in his car, please may I use yours?" I felt so small and stupid as the words came out.

"Of course you can, please, come through to the kitchen; I will make you a drink" I was lucky, the man at this house was friendly. He made me a coffee, listened to my woes, and warned me that a young lady shouldn't really be going around knocking on peoples doors, it was dangerous. I agreed with him, and admitted that I felt embarrassed of my behaviour.

I dialled Marks mobile number, I knew it from memory. He didn't answer. I dialled it again, 5 times I let it go to answerphone, and finally he picked up.

"Hello?" he was curious over the unknown number "Mark it's me, please can you come and pick me up so I can go with you, we need to talk" I tried to get as much out as fast as I could, before he could possibly cut me off, shouting over the top of me like I expected him to.

"No Ruth, I can't and I won't. I am leaving the house now to go to the tattoo parlour. I don't want to see you and I don't want you to come with me, I can't be doing with you at all at the moment."

"But what will I do, I'm stuck here, how can I get back Mark?."

"That's your problem; I will leave you a key outside the house. Maybe it will give you some time to think about your actions."

With that he hung up on me. I was the child disciplined by the parent.

Then I got to experience the further humiliation of crying again in front of the horrified old man, who couldn't understand why Mark wouldn't come and get me, and passed me tissues as I wailed, out of despair and discomfort to be in this ridiculous scenario.

There was one saving grace. The lovely old man's wife was disabled, and returning back from her bingo session in a taxi, and when it dropped her off outside, I swapped with her and the old man got the driver to take me to my house.

"Now are you sure you don't need any money?" He asked kindly "No, it's fine, I have some at my house, you have done enough for me already, thank you."

"OK Gal, well it's none of my business, but I think a pretty little thing like you can do better and should be kept care of" I smiled at back at him through the glass as the car pulled away.

I felt so much relief as I got dropped off at my own front door and went under a big rock for the key.

Once I was back in the safety of my own home I sat at the bottom of the stairs with the dogs.

I stared into space thinking. Boundaries had been crossed that day, and this was my fault. I decided I wouldn't admit to that. The dimensions of our relationship had changed. There was very little compromise left in either of us.

Xmas 2010

We were fast heading towards Christmas, and in the last few days of work before we broke up, I was out with my boss visiting clients.

We stopped to get some lunch at a cafe on the way back to the office.

Sat on bar stools eating burgers and supping on chocolate milkshake we were just chatting.

"I think you are very trusting to have taken Mark back the way you have and made a go of things" It felt like he was probing for more details. I felt myself bristle.

"Yes, well, we just need some space and time" I wasn't giving much thought to what he was saying, it sounded as if he was digging for gossip and I wasn't really that interested in sharing.

"I am just telling you this as a friend Ruth, but have you seen what he said on Facebook about Jackie?"

"What are you on about John?" suddenly I was listening, irritated to have been drawn but my interest sparked. The suggestion of trouble threatening to spoil my mood.

Johns beckoned to his car, relishing the concept of storytelling on the journey. His explanation to me was mostly built around social media, and how Mark kept commenting on things which Jackie had posted, and some of it was a little too personal, adding that he believed that they texted each other all the time. John was describing some fairly filthy content and I began to feel little prickles as all the hairs on my neck stood on end.

I sat quietly in the passenger seat my head in a spin, voices already whispering. In reality I decided that I doubted if what he was saying was even true, but if it were, I further doubted whether there was any intent for them to start seeing each other.

John knew Jackie because she had baby sat for his children and done some cleaning at his house. That was how Mark and I had come to meet her; she frequently popped into the office, and was often invited on work nights out and events. As far as I knew, Jackie was happily settled down with her new boyfriend.

What was bothering me was based on a level of trust. Here I was again finding out from my boss that my husband appeared to be playing around, how I could not fulfil his needs, and everyone could see this except me, shielded in my little self-created bubble.

I didn't want the outside world to know how weak my marriage was.

I sent Mark a text "What is going on with you and Jackie? John has been telling me things."

Instantly the reply.

"Nothing is going on, ignore that poisonous bastard, I will explain to you when we get home from work tonight."

The remainder of my day was not productive. Something wasn't right, I felt creepy and unsettled.

After I had left the office I went straight to the yard, I checked my phone when I got there, as I always did. I had a text from an unknown number. I took deep breaths and held the car door to steady myself as I read in the dark. Alone.

"Ruth its Jackie. I have spoken to Mark. I have heard what John has been saying to you and it is malicious. Mark and I do text each other and I guess he has said some silly things , but believe me and trust me woman to woman, I would not do that to you, I've had it done to me before and I know how much it hurt. Call me later if you like? But you don't have to."

I felt a little calmer, I could almost get air in and out of my lungs. I decided that I would ring her when I got home. It was bitterly cold again that night and the frost felt like it was after me. I got lazer settled and left. Mark wasn't in the house when I got home so I called Jackie straightaway.

"Ruth I don't know what John's game is to be honest, he is stirring up trouble but I don't know why he is doing it. My ex-husband messed around with other women, and I know how it felt, so I wouldn't do that to you, or in fact to any woman but if you don't believe me then at least believe Mark. He is a good man."

She sounded sincere enough. I did believe her. But how did I explain my inside feelings to anyone. Cheating was one thing. Hurtful and sneaky. But making the comments he had made about her on a public forum and then also texting her all the time? It was almost pathetic. As if he was obsessing about her and she wasn't that interested or didn't seem to be. Meanwhile I felt as if everyone knew what I suspected to be the truth. Mark may as well have made a status update himself "hey everyone, my wife doesn't interest me anymore, so I run around after every attractive woman I meet ."

I sat in in the dark in the lounge for a while after I had finished speaking to Jackie. Nothing really made sense to me anymore. It seemed like there were skeletons in everyone's wardrobes these days...once again my personal life had become like a soap opera and friends and colleagues had gotten involved.

Mark arrived home and banged the front door, and charged into the lounge "I have every mind to ring that conniving git" he spat. He was angry "Trying to upset you like this, all because of what happened between me and Jane before I expect, he is making a mountain out of a molehill, I swear nothing is going in between me and Jackie."

I looked at him. He was stood in the hallway. His shoulders squared up his brow in a frown and his cheeks were slightly red from the shouting. Like he wanted a fight. But not with me. Maybe inner demons.

We didn't talk much more. We ate some dinner and sat on the sofa together, Mark with his laptop on his knee, with his phone next to him, king of his virtual friends.

I went upstairs and sat on the edge of the bed in the spare room and called Kate.

"The thing is, I know he isn't really that bothered about Jackie, but he doesn't make any effort towards wanting to be with me. I feel like I am not enough for him. When he said that time I could never be what he wanted. He is right."

As ever, Kate was careful not to pass judgement.

"Wait until you get some time off together over Christmas Ruth, I am sure that things will change when you both have a break, it's been intense for you these last few months."

Kate was right. A day or two later we broke up for Christmas. Mark and I did spend some time together over the break. We went walking with the dogs, and he tolerated the cold and come over to the yard with me to see Lazer. We visited family, his and mine. We celebrated with large dinners, presents and all the usual festivities.

We sat down one evening to watch a film, poured some glasses of wine and sat together, for once there wasn't the constant sound of his phone bing bonging and the laptop stayed down the side of the sofa.

The film was good. It was about two lovers who shared so much feeling and passion for each other. Unfortunately though the main male character dies in this film. The woman has to accept that she loved a great man, and embrace what she had with him once he is gone.

After the film had finished I had a really strange sensation. It was like I knew mine and Marks life together would never be like that again. Like we had crossed over a line that we couldn't seem to reverse, there was no way back to how things had been before he left me. Even when on the face of things our relationship seemed intact, I knew that in reality it was falling to pieces.

I wandered into the kitchen and put some dishes into the sink and finished the last of the deep red wine off. I must have been staring into space when Mark came into the kitchen.

"What's the matter Ruth?" he asked concerned

I realised that I was standing looking out of the kitchen window into the night darkness, and tears were streaming down my face and my fists were clenched into little balls.

"I just realised you can't make someone love you. If they do then that's one thing, but if they don't you can't make them" I put my hands to my face.

Mark moved swiftly across the kitchen and wrapped me up in his arms. Squeezing my shoulders. But this was not the hug of a lover, it resembled the sort of strong yet friendly hug I might get from one of my brothers. Mark said nothing. He agreed with what I was saying. He just wasn't brave enough to answer.

There we stood in the kitchen in a silent embrace, neither of us wanting to take the conversation any further.

Yet later on when we were getting ready to turn in for the night, we still walked around our bedroom naked and snuggled up together in the same bed. These confusing messages felt like they would go on for an eternity.

The following day was one of quiet and pensive behaviour from Mark. I had got to the stage where I dare not ask him what was wrong, and he wasn't forthcoming. He was further withdrawn into his socialising with people on the laptop and the phone…that was what his world revolved around. This and his garage gym. That was all. I may as well not have existed

I had always felt when Mark had left me that I didn't know the man he had become. But by the end of 2010 I felt as though he was different again. I didn't know this man either. He was quiet and withdrawn, and showed little emotion. He didn't seem to want to go anywhere or do anything together. There was no play fighting or kissing. There were no open signs of affection.

I was getting more and more worried that he was suffering from depression.

One evening whilst he was downstairs with the tv blaring away, his laptop and phone at the ready I went quietly upstairs and shut myself into my walk-in wardrobe and called the counselling service.

I sat amongst striped shirts and flowered dresses and explained everything to the man on the other end of the line.

"I feel like I'm going mad, I really do, it's like only I can see it, the changes in him and his behaviour, but then because only I can see it I really do feel like perhaps it is me" I blabbered at him "I am really worried about him. I worry all the time that he is going to do something drastic because he is so unhappy, like hurt himself."

"It's OK, I actually don't think you are going mad at all, we have talked about how he has changed and I do believe you, and I do think something is wrong with Mark, and I think he is probably suffering. The good news is that he has you to look after him. You must urge him to seek professional help."

After I had spoken further to the councillor I spent a little while letting my eyes dry, and hoping my face looked less puffy. I was still sat on the floor, running my fingers through the thick black carpet in the walk in wardrobe, and as far as I was aware Mark had not moved from downstairs.

New year 2011

The days that followed me calling the counselling service were difficult. I told Mark that I had called them. I explained to him that I thought he needed professional help. I urged him that I felt like something was wrong but he wasn't telling me what it was.

I didn't go into the details. Not telling him that I thought he had become obsessed with social networking sites, and weight training and all the other things that went around and around in my head. I thought it may have angered him and pushed him over the edge. When Mark got angry there was no reasoning with him, so I tried hard to avoid that.

Instead I just tried to gently push him towards going to the doctors and telling them he wasn't happy. But he flatly refused, and said that there was nothing wrong with him. It was me. I was the only one who thought he was out of character.

Christmas festivities soon ended and I felt relieved. It had been hard work putting on a brave face in front of both families amongst all of the angst that I felt inside. I went from moments of thinking things were going to come good again, to moments of absolute despair.

I wondered whether anyone else noticed Marks odd behaviour, or was it just me. And therefore, was it actually me that was slowly going insane?

I didn't tell anyone about the evening we had watched that film, or that I had called the counselling service. I came to the conclusion that everything I was thinking should get shut in that mental drawer I had created. So I locked away my fears about Marks stream of admirers, and shut away any more thoughts about his odd, pensive behaviour. We needed to move on.

Mark and I made the decision to welcome the New Year in on our own. We had previously planned to go to Kate and Charles for the festivities, but as it got closer to leaving to make the journey a thick blanket of fog had descended over the UK and Mark decided he didn't fancy driving through hours of it. But he fog wasn't just outside.

I was disappointed as I called off various pet sitters and went last minute shopping for some supper. I cooked a special meal for us and we had some champagne. Tried to plough on as normal.

As we opened the dining room patio at midnight we could see and hear fireworks for miles around us as we chinked our glasses.

It was a pleasant evening, I can't say it wasn't, and if I was a person on the outside of the glass, looking in to the room as we watched those fireworks, they would have seen a couple, close together, smiling and sipping champagne.

But as I looked up into Marks eyes I knew he wasn't really with me.

He was there in body gently holding me, but in his mind he had already left and gone someplace else.

The day of the accident

I was at the stable yard. It was the last day of the Christmas break, and I had just brought Lazer into her stable and bedded her down for the night. I was sweeping the concrete hard standing. There was a really icy, biting wind. The dogs were running around playing with sticks.

My mobile was ringing from deep within my pocket; I struggled to answer it with two pairs of gloves on, digging it out from the depth of my duck down coat.

"Ruth, I think I have written the car off" It was Mark, he sounded shaken.

"Are you hurt?" I asked him, immediately feeling panicked "Where are you Mark?."

He explained to me that he was only a few miles from our village, and he thought he had some glass in his hands, but other than that he was ok.

I petted Lazer, checked her stable door was double locked, and rushed both dogs into the back of the truck. I drove as fast as I could to the location he had given me.

But I didn't need to wonder about where Mark and the car were. As I came around the corner a thick sea of blue flashing lights lined the side of the road.

I could see the back end of the evolution. It was sat upright in a farmer's field. Not a single panel was left clean. It was smashed on all sides and the roof, covered in mud, debris and plants and the exhaust was somehow pointing out of the front of the car.

I parked up behind one of the ambulances. Thinking about a television programme I had watched once where a woman's son had called her to say he had an accident but he was ok, but then seconds after that he blacked out and died. Although the sirens were blaring and this was a busy main road all I could hear was my own heart pumping in my ears. I was shacking all over as I clambered out of the truck.

A policeman walked towards me.

"Who are you?"

"I'm Ruth Shaw, I'm Marks wife, I need to see him."

"I can't let you see him at the moment I am afraid to say. I promise you that he is not seriously hurt, they are just checking him over in the ambulance, he has glass in his hands and maybe in his eye but no serious injuries, which judging by the car, is nothing short of a miracle."

As the officer was talking to me we had started to walk together towards the evo.

I have never seen a vehicle up that close with so much damage. It was as if giant hands had grabbed it, lifted it from the road and crushed it up. Fortunately the driver's side hadn't seen much impact. Although there was glass everywhere, the worse damage was on the passengers side and the rear of the car.

I felt bile in my throat as I looked at passenger seat, my usual spot. Maybe I wouldn't have been so lucky.

Another officer came storming over to us purposefully and the man who I was already talking to introduced him as his partner.

"Walk this way with me and I want to show you something."

I followed them to where some large tyre shaped, dark streaks crossed over from the right of the road, towards oncoming traffic, and then back toward the left, and then a large hole in the hedge and undergrowth.

"You will see from these marks on the road, that had anyone been coming the other way Mark would have definitely hit them. And had this been the case we would be most likely looking at multiple fatalities."

His words sounded surreal to me. He went on.

"Could have been a mother with children on the way back from a day out, could have been any of us, could have even been you. And whoever he hit , their family's would be pressing for death by dangerous driving. I don't need to tell you more about this do I?" He was condescending, but he was right.

"You certainly don't need to tell me about it!" I shouted angrily at the policemen. "Do you think I don't know what could have happened here? I know I could have been being called to view his body, or deal with relatives whose loved ones he had taken, you don't need to preach to me about it."

"I just think you need to understand. Before we came here this evening we were at another accident and the consequences of someone's reckless actions were far worse. And I am going to personally try and see to it that your husband is prosecuted."

The less angry policeman lead me back towards the ambulance.

"Sorry love, but we don't like dealing with men like your husband."

At this point Mark stepped out of the back of the ambulance.

"Hi, how are you?" He smiled at me. Like this has all just some big jolly joke, and I didn't know if he was in shock, or if he had totally lost the plot. He seemed to have no comprehension of what was going on around him.

He thrust his wallet and his phone at me.

"I have to stay in the ambulance with them, if you can follow us to the hospital then you can come into A and E and sit with me."

I looked from Mark, and his cold unfeeling eyes, the way he stood tall, like he had done no wrong, to the policemen, and to the ambulance crew drivers.

The cold shiver crept up my spine and into my neck as I felt myself start to prickle and tremble.

I drove along behind the ambulance. It was going slowly and I mostly knew the roads anyway. The dogs were crying, sat in the back of my truck. They were cold, wet and muddy and didn't realise what was going on. I didn't understand how we all got here either. I managed to keep a hold of the steering wheel with my shaking hands. My mouth was so dry I could barely swallow. I felt sick and dizzy and like there was no clean air to breathe. Although it was bitterly cold I had to open a window.

I thought about Marks recent state of mind. It was possible that he had this accident on purpose. A fast driver Mark had always been. But a careless driver no. He was experienced behind the wheel of performance vehicles. A horrid thought went across my mind, could this actually be what he had wanted to happen. That he didn't want to be saved, didn't want to hit the gap in the hedge and sail through the air and somehow end up relatively unhurt? I pushed the thought to the back of my mind, putting it away to deal with it later.

I parked the truck up in the hospital car park and left the windows venting so the dogs had some air.

Mark was being admitted by the triage team when I walked through the main doors. He was then given a place to sit and wait. I sat with him. I gave Mark his phone back.

"Come on Ruth, it's all going to be alright you know!" he laughed and gave me a big bear hug. Then he was on his phone. Back to his people.

We sat and chatted quietly, Mark munching on chocolate at what looked like the onset of a diabetic hypo. My phone started ringing. I walked outside of the reception area to answer.

"Ruth, its Carol, Mark has put pictures and comments on a social networking site. He has given all the details of the accident. It's not funny and he will get into even more trouble, please get him to take them down!" She sounded frustrated and upset. I could hear Patrick shouting angrily in the back ground. As an ex-police officer he knew all too well this could lead to prosecution. Blatant disregard for the situation, and turning it into a circus would not go in Marks favour.

"I will try, but he is just not himself, I can't really explain." Now wasn't the time to express my inner thoughts to Carol.

"I know Ruth, I know, but please tell him that his Dad tells him to get them down straight away, especially with what the police said about charges."

When I went back to the waiting area Mark predictably said that he couldn't understand what all the fuss was about, and all though he protested, he did agree to take the pictures and comments away from the public eye.

Sometime later a doctor fished the little bits of glass out of Mark eyes and dressed his hands. We were released from the A and E department for which I was grateful.

When we got back to the house, his brother, Martyn was waiting outside in his car. They went together back to the evolution, they needed to remove all the CDs and in car entertainment so it didn't get stolen from the crash site.

Whist they were out I seized the opportunity to call Kate. I needed to speak to someone who was grounded.

"Oh my god Ruth, do you think he was trying to do himself in?" she exclaimed.

"I just don't know Kate, but I think it is unlikely, because I think he would be dead if he had wanted to be. I could see how fast he had been going. It's like he was racing against an invisible version of himself."

I felt breathless as I continued. "I just don't know what to do anymore. I feel so desperate, I don't know him, I don't know if I even want to know him, the harder I try the further away he gets and I can't reach him anymore" I was babbling away to myself as much as to Kate.

"I feel like I am on a roundabout. If I go straight on Mark and I stay together, we might be happy, we might not, and at the moment we certainly are not. If I turn right and leave him then I lose all that I know and I am scared. If I turn left, well, there is no left, there are no other options! I just keep going around and around, I don't know what to do anymore. When we were apart it killed me, but being with him when he doesn't love me, it's just killing me more. He could have died today!"

"Oh Ruth, I am so sorry. I don't know what to tell you to do at all" Kate whispered.

I wish she was there with me. So I could just cry on her.

Later when Mark was back from salvaging things out of his car we sat down in the lounge together and talked for a while. I told him what the police said to me, that they were after him and were going to press charges .He told me that he would have to go in to the station and have a proper interview about what had happened.

I looked at his face. He looked like the traumatised version of himself now. He wasn't angry. He looked worried and scared. He got up and walked out of the lounge to the kitchen and was gone for what felt like forever. I slowly followed him.

Mark was stood with his head in his hands, his elbows propped on the worktops and his laptop in front of him. He was just staring at the screen. He looked miserable.

"Mark, can I do anything?" I moved towards him and tried to wrap him in my arms, but he gently wriggled away.

"When I think about what could have happened Ruth, and what could have been. I almost don't know why I am still here. I have been so very lucky."

Realisation was starting to sneak into Marks mind, making him think differently. The bravado and anger had gone and been replaced with a quieter more thoughtful man.

But for all the things he was feeling, he still couldn't quite let me in, and I felt powerless to help.

As I tried to sleep that night a dark thought entered my head. If Mark had died in the accident he would have died the man I and loved and adored, and I would miss him so terribly. But would that be better being with a man I didn't feel I knew anymore? And would it be easier to cope with him dead than not loving me anymore. I felt instantly guilty and locked the thought in the mental drawer with all of the others.

An evening at the pub

We both went back to work the day after Marks car accident. We were busy in our respective jobs. We fell back into our routines. Working long hours, Mark training in the garage, I would go to the yard in the evenings whilst he walked the dogs.

I was still not able to put my fears aside. On the face of the relationship we were a normal couple. Friends and family perhaps considered that we had had a blip, and now things were as they always had been. Only I knew different. The silence that had fallen between us. The conversations that were left alone. His harem of followers, who I hated. The way when he looked at me I knew it wasn't love; I don't think it was even contentment any more by that time.

The more I considered Marks growing unusual behaviour, the more I also began to think it was me, a problem in my head.

I felt a desperate feeling of failure descending over me. Mark needed help and I couldn't seem to save him, and I was slowly sinking too. We were falling into a pit of depression.

We really needed to talk. If I could only find a way to make the conversations come. I suggested we went out for tea one night, maybe in a relaxed atmosphere he would finally open up?

We went to a busy pub a few villages away. It was bright and busy, so we were free to chatter without really being heard in all of the bustle.Perfect.

Our main courses were on the table in front of us and we were eating like we had never been fed. I was thinking about asking something and I took the plunge.

"Shall we book a holiday Mark? Sometime soon, give us some time alone? A chance to talk properly"

Mark looked up from his dinner and his phone and glared at me.

"No Ruth, I don't think that's a good idea" there was no enthusiasm in his voice, and I was taken aback.

"Come on, even if it's just a week somewhere, I know you worry about the money but we can get a late deal, I think it's perhaps what we need. Just you and I?"

"No Ruth, that's not really it. I can't go away with you; I can't be away with just you. I need my other distractions and things; I don't really want to go on holiday with you."

I swallowed the lump of food I had been chewing on for the last few moments; it was almost as if it had turned to concrete in my mouth and set solid. I sat looking around me at this room full of apparently happy people; I didn't want them to know how crushed I was. How I felt like I was dying inside. The tears were trying to prick into my eyes and the strength was leaving my body. A cold trickle of sweat ran down the back of my neck. I shivered. But I wouldn't give in. I couldn't show these onlookers that I was ruined, and I wouldn't show Mark either.

I pushed the remainder of my food around my plate creatively so it looked like I had eaten more. I prayed for the waitress to come and clean up quickly, so I could pay her, and we could leave. After what felt like and eternity the time came and I drove us home.

Mark went straight upstairs to get in the shower. He had said nothing to me on our journey or when we got back. He just stared at his phone intensely.

Whilst Mark was upstairs I sat in the dark on the sofa and let the tears come. Until they wouldn't stop and I cried until I was almost sick.

I heard Marks footsteps go down the stairs and into the kitchen, so I hastily moved from the lounge to the bedroom, so he couldn't see me, and my red face, and the fact I could barely carry myself.

I shut myself in the walk-in wardrobe and called Kate.

"It's all gone wrong Kate. I asked him about a holiday, but he won't do it, he says he doesn't want to go away with me, he doesn't want a holiday, and he needs his distractions."

"Oh Ruth, I am so sorry, I thought that would have been a good idea."

"I am back on the roundabout again Kate. I feel like I can't make things right. I wanted to take him away from all of his worries and problems so it would just be us and see what happened, even if we had come back separated we would have tried, but he doesn't even want to try. So if I can't go straight on then I have to go right, and I just don't know if I am strong enough. I'm exhausted, I've got nothing left."

"Shush" Kate said calmly "Get a shower and go to bed and let him think on what he has said. Please try and get some sleep. I love you Ruth."

"Love you too."

And I tried, I really did. Sleep eventually silenced my roundabout demons that night, and I spent some more days locking my feelings back in their drawer, where they couldn't hurt me.

Rock bottom

I started to spiral.

Having had the roundabout experience, the feelings of desperation came more every day, and the visit to the pub had put a tin lid on things.

I caught a virus. Normally I would dose myself up with medicines and head to work but instead I gave in to illness and called in sick. I spent all day on the sofa surrounded by the dogs and the cat, wrapped in duvets, feeling cold and achy. I spent a lot of time watching the TV. I mean literally watching it. I was not really participating in the content; instead I was just staring in to space, mildly interested from time to time in what was happening on the screen.

On my second day of being in my pyjamas I was once again glued to the sofa, in my sweaty blankets when Mark came home from work in the middle of the day.

I was surprised to see him.

"What's up?" I croaked

"I was out checking up on a project I was running and Liam called me and asked to meet me here."

Mark was running several large jobs at that time and as the contracts manager it was his job to keep the staff and the customers satisfied. Liam was Marks boss. Usually if they met it was at the office, and I was wondering why Liam had chosen to meet Mark at our house. I could tell Mark was puzzled too.

We didn't have to wait any longer though because 5 minutes after Mark had arrived Liam turned up.

He came into the lounge.

"Hi, how are you?" I asked, looking at him he didn't seem to be able to keep still, and had a nervous energy about him.

"Better than you by the looks of things" he joked.

Mark and Liam went outside with coffees and Liam lit a cigarette. The dogs pestered them with toys to throw. I couldn't hear what was being said as the patio door had been shut. I wondered curiously what was going on. I looked at them, they were both very sombre, but neither of them looked angry.

I lay back on the sofa and closed my eyes and drifted into a cold fuelled sleep.

"Bye Ruth" the front door was slamming and Liam was leaving. I jolted awake and sat upright again.

Mark came and sat on the end of my blanket, gently moving my feet out of the way so he could sit.

"The company went under this morning" he said quietly

"I have to go and tell all the lads they don't have jobs. I have to stop the major projects and then later I will have to help Liam with some other things."

His voice was small, almost whispering as he spoke.

"I'm so sorry Mark" my voice also quiet, I didn't know what to say.

"I knew things weren't great, but I didn't think they were this bad."

"Liam has plans for me and some of the longer term blokes, he thinks he has found employment for most long term people, it's important to him."

"My van will have to go, and so will the stock in the garage" Mark was staring into space.

Like he wasn't even in the lounge, he had gone to another place.

"Don't wait up for me tonight Ruth; there will be lots I have to take care of."

I wanted to hug him. I wanted to kiss him. I wanted to hold him and try and take away some of the pain. I wanted to ask him questions about what he thought he would do. There were so many things I wanted to say and do, but I couldn't, Mark had shut down, he didn't want my help. He wanted to walk this journey alone.

He left the room and I heard him close the front door.

So that was it then. This was what rock bottom felt like.

Broken

It was Friday evening and I was glad for the weekends arrival.

Mark had for once agreed that we could go on a walk together. We walked down the trail, side by side in the pitch black. There was a biting cold wind, and I was glad of my layers, pulling my hat down as the cold tried to get in my ears.

It was hard to know what to talk about .A million unsaid words hung in the small space between us. The silence far more terrifying than the darkness.

If we talked about how his company had gone bust, and all the trauma that the individual people were facing, Mark would talk to a point but then he would shut down. If we talked about my work then I got angry, because I wasn't happy there, but at least I still had a job. Guilt kept me away from that topic. We did talk about work briefly, but then we hastily moved onto other people, friends, safer subjects.

My inner curiosity was on the go though, and as Mark was talking about some friends who had split up a few years back and both re-married, I had the lead needed to ask him some questions.

"Do you think that if we split up, that I would get married again?"

"Oh yes, definitely."

"Do you think you would?"

"I don't know I'm not sure."

"And if I was married to someone else do you think I would have children with them?"

"I think you might Ruth yes."

"And what about you?"

"No, I don't think so" he said sadly.

And then we carried on trudging in silence, an empty space between us where we would have once held hands, and the moonlight casting shadows on our separate figures.

Adjusting, I walked slightly behind Mark, an aching in my heart as it felt like it was slowly disintegrating.

Because I had wanted him to say, don't be silly Ruth, we won't split up, we will stay together, and we are married, and maybe one day we will have children. I wanted him to look to his future and my future and to see them together as a joint entity. But his answers to my questions told a thousand tales.

Back at the house I felt broken. Sapped. Empty. All I could manage to do was sit on the heated kitchen floor with my legs crossed. My mouth dry and the start of the cold feeling pouring down my neck.

"What's up Ruth? You want me to make tea?" He seemed to be unaware of my fragile state.

"Yea, that would be nice" I couldn't even raise my head to look at him. Like a puppet whose strings had been cut, I felt as if my arms and legs were limp.

Eventually I did manage to move and took off my boots and coat. I sat at the foot of the stairs for a while, whilst Mark cooked the dinner.

I thought about calling Kate. But I didn't need to this time. I knew that there wasn't a roundabout anymore. There was only one road left for me to take.

The end

It was a Sunday morning. I had got up and been to let Lazer out of her stable and mucked her out, come home and Mark and I had breakfast together.

Once we had finished and the dirty plates and cups were in the dishwasher I wondered what Mark had planned for the day.

He was in the dining room, wearing his moleskins and a jumper and was clearly getting ready to go for a walk.

"Are you about to take the dogs out?" I asked, starting to change my own socks, planning to join them.

Yes, I am going up into the woods on the top of the hill" His tone seemed plain.

"Great stuff, can I can come?"

"No, not really Ruth, I am going alone" No Movement in his voice. Adamant.

He wouldn't even turn around to look at my face.

I went through many reasons in my head as to why he might not want me there, was it because I walked too slowly? Was it because he wanted time alone? Or was he going to call someone whilst he was up in the woods or maybe he was going to meet someone whilst he was up there, all the different connotations spun around in my head.

My body was overwhelmed by a crushing sensation. Like I was not able to breathe because I couldn't actually inhale, like all of my limbs and organs were slowly being squashed as Mark crushed them with invisible fingers.

I was defeated. I walked slowly from the kitchen to the utility room. My body felt so heavy, like I couldn't carry it. The shiny glints of brass on the work top caught my eye. Barney and Teddy were in that room out of the way after Mark complained when they were in the dining room. I went over to the caskets. I had a photo album on top of Barneys, from a time before digital cameras were available.

I opened the album. I was there with Barney in loads of photographs, but my favourite was us galloping through the trees. His orange main and tail streaking out behind him, nostrils flared, going as fast as his legs would take him. I am on board smiling, leant slightly forward up out of the saddle like a jockey, my blonde mane trailing behind me also. I could still remember how moving at that speed made my eyes water so much that I could barely see, but I wasn't afraid. I was brave. I was 16 years old and I was afraid of nothing when that picture was taken.

I closed the album. I thought about the brave girl who was only 16 years old, who was scared of nothing because the world hadn't thrown anything at her to cause fear yet. I thought of how strong she was, ready to take on anything, every ambition and aspiration she could have if she wanted it and everything to experience. Her life ahead of her.

I walked calmly from the utility to the hall way, up the stairs and to the spare room. I went over to the chest of drawers and I took out my jewellery boxes.

I took out the navy textured box, which had 'Harrisons' inscribed in gold italics on the lid.

I smiled with fond memories of the day when Mark and I had stood in the jewellers, in the Dominican Republic, choosing the Gold and Platinum bands. The assistant had explained to us where each ring was from, and how they would have to alter mine to get it to fit my small finger. How mine had sat in the box inside Marks. So safe.

I snapped myself back into reality. I gently eased my wedding ring off my finger and nestled it in its box.

I went out of the spare room and back down the stairs to the lounge, where Mark was sat on the sofa staring at the wall.

'My wedding ring is back in its box. Please can you put your ring in this box now?'

As I spoke there was a lump in my throat so big I that I could barely speak. But I overcame.

"I can Ruth, but why?"

"Because I have the bollocks to do this Mark, I have the balls to finish what you couldn't. It's all over. Take off your ring and put it in this box." I looked around the room and pointed "I will take all of these wedding photographs down, I will take all of our photographs down. I will get the house on to the market, and I will go to the solicitors and put an end to all of this misery."

Mark looked at me, with his face pale, he had no words, but I had many more for him.

"Thing is Mark I deserve better than this. I deserve someone who wants to be with me, who shows it to me and means it. I deserve a partner who wants to walk the dogs with me on a Sunday, who is prepared to help me with the horses from time to time, a man who would like to go on holiday with me. Who wants to cherish me and share every moment with me? I deserve more. I deserve better. I deserve to be everything to somebody."

The cold feeling, the aching all over my body and the exhausted feeling I was being crushed from inside out had been alleviated by a new found anger.

I stormed into the dining room, where the empty bottle of champagne sat that we had at new year, a candle in the top of it as a decoration.

"This can go outside, I am throwing this in the bin, because it wasn't a happy new year at all was it!"

I raged, smashing things into the bin, and storming back into the lounge.

"You can get out of my bed and my room too Mark. I don't want to share them with you anymore. It's quite clear it doesn't mean to you what it should."

I thundered around the house taking down every picture of us together.

Pictures of us on holiday, at the beach, getting married, with the pets, all of those happy memories. But that's all they were. They were just places we had been. And there wouldn't be any more of them. As I threw them all into a box and shut the lid I was trying to block them away.

We spoke no more. There was nothing else to say.

I drove to the yard as Mark left the house with the dogs.

From the safety of Lazers stable I cried my heart out until I vomited and choked. For all of my bravado back at the house, now the emotions could come. Crushed by Marks lack of response, there was no begging or pleading with me not to do this. Only a silent and sad agreement. He wanted this too. All along. He just hadn't had the conviction.

I called Carol and I called Mum.

They both offered to drive over, or speak to Mark or anything to try and repair the situation. But I didn't want that, not this time. I knew that it was over. I had meant every word that I said. I did deserve better, and I had chosen to save myself from what had become a torturous existence.

After I hung up from Mum I got a text from Mark.

'I am so sorry about what has happened and what I have done Ruth. I have let problems build up all of my life and not talked about them. It feels like I buried everything under the carpet and now it's made a big lump, and I have fallen over it and banged my head and I cannot get up'

I read it several times.

I knew Mark was right.

That day I had saved two people.

No matter how much him leaving me had killed me over and over again, until I thought I couldn't take any more, it had hurt so much more being in a relationship where I didn't feel loved or wanted, and we weren't able to make each other happy anymore. And no matter how much it hurt inside, almost until it felt as if my heart had shattered into thousands of tiny pieces that I could never pick up again, when I said those words back at the house. They had to be said.

And I had to set us both free.

Conclusion

Mark and I continued to live together in our house for about another year.

At first this arrangement was very hard work for us. I didn't adapt very well to Mark and I eating separately, and being in the house together but not actually talking to each other or interacting. It's peculiar after 12 years of considering another person and their wishes and then not having to include them in day to day life.

Mark started a relationship with Rebecca within a few days of ours ending. I was gutted and considered it had probably been brewing for the last few months we were together.

I have my suspicions that whilst Mark and I were still together he was seeing several other women. I also found a sim card on top of a wardrobe , which contained many naked pictures of what I assume where his harem of followers. The dates on the pictures were all within the time that we were back together and trying to make things work.

Additionally I discovered on the day of Marks accident there were reasons as to why he came off the road at such high speed, and behaved in such a dangerous manner. I only hope the sex was worth the horrendous risks that were taken with not just two people's life's but those around them.

Either way I have come to my own conclusions. But I don't have to worry about these things anymore. If I can't be everything to my life partner then I would rather be nothing to them at all.

I filed for divorce against Mark based on irreconcilable differences.

A year later our house finally sold and another family lives there.

The story I have written started years ago. I was not strong enough to write it at the time that the events were happening.

I cannot begin to explain the emotional pain that I went through, although I know all who read this and have been through a similar experience won't need any explanation.

When Mark came back, if he had been fully committed to making our relationship work then perhaps I could have offered him full and total forgiveness, but possibly a small part of me knew even then that this was just not the case.

I really meant what I said; when Mark had his accident I would have easily accepted him being dead over not loving me or caring for me anymore.

But Kate's words were so true, I had to go through all of this to come out at the other side, and having done that I feel victorious and all sense of malice left me a long time ago.

Joanna's words are true too. I did fall in love and meet someone very special again. But I kept a little bit back, in a safe place, to make sure I survive.

I often think about me, the 16 year old girl in the photograph, with her whole life ahead of her, but actually it was the same when I was 30, and I hope it continues. There were many doors left open for me, I just had to be brave enough to go through them.

The Future (in brief!)

I had new found confidence to go out and meet people, some who I knew and some who I was yet to meet. I took great enjoyment from amazing nights out and threw myself into being the centre of attention again.

Mum was correct, I really did have men falling at my feet. After all those years the dating game was a source of fascination, un-nerving yet thrilling.

Then when I was least expecting, I met up with someone who I had not seen for years. The boy I had once known has turned into a wonderful man. Realising that I was still somewhat broken he healed my wounds.

I joined a new training programme with Lazer. She is still a confident and dominant mare. She will of course always be large. But I am now able to lead her and stay in control of her. I have been able to build a partnership with my horse which I never dreamed was possible.

I quit my job working with John and Jane. The less said about them and their company the better. I had some months off to write the story you are now reading! I ended up with 3 excellent offers of employment and chose what I felt was the best fit for me and my future.

All of these things I have written about so briefly are perfectly possible. So if you read this book as you are going through something similar, I hope it helps you get through the hardest times of your life.

One thing is for sure, you will be stronger than you could possibly think. And you will get through. With the help of your family and friends you will come out at the other side. And it will be worth it.

Oh yes, and Mark, you said you would make me great one day. Looks like you finally did.

A note about name changes

You will, no doubt, have noticed by now that this book appears to be about a couple called Ruth and Mark, and their families.

There is no mystery. I am Ruth. Ruth is the middle name, given to me by my parents.

I have changed names when writing and developing this book, to protect the identities of some individuals, at their request.

Printed in Great Britain
by Amazon